SWIMMING UPSTREAM

Anthony Fingleton was born in Brisbane in 1940,
graduated from Harvard in 1967 and now lives in
New York City. He has worked for many years as
a screenwriter and producer in movies and television.
He is married and has two adult daughters.

swimming
upstream

anthony fingleton

TEXT PUBLISHING MELBOURNE AUSTRALIA

The Text Publishing Company
171 La Trobe Street
Melbourne Victoria 3000
Australia

This edition published 2003
Printed and bound by Griffin Press
Designed by Chong Weng-ho
Typeset in 10.8/16.5 Sabon by J & M Typesetting

National Library of Australia
Cataloguing-in-Publication data:
  Fingleton, Anthony, 1940- .
  Swimming upstream.

ISBN 1 877008 29 X.

1. Fingleton, Anthony, 1940- . 2. Swimmers - Australia - Biography. I. Title.

797.21092

To my sister, Diane,
whose anguish over our young lives
spurred the writing of this book and the
subsequent movie.
Her courage and success are an inspiration to me.

part 1

DORA AND HAROLD FINGLETON WITH THEIR FAMILY, AROUND 1950.
FROM LEFT: JOHN, RONALD, DIANE, TONY, HAROLD JNR

chapter 1

It's hot in Queensland during the summer months, really hot. But that never bothered us. We coped with that heat in a way that would shape our lives forever. It would send us on paths that we could not possibly have imagined. What we became was due in large part to the fact that we lived a minute from the Spring Hill Baths.

I was one of five Fingleton children. Harold Junior was born in 1939. I came along eighteen months later in 1940. There was a gap of three years due to a miscarriage until John was born in 1943, another son Ronald in 1945 and, in 1947, my mother Dora got the daughter she so desperately wanted when Diane was born.

During the six to eight weeks of summer holidays, we spent the greater part of our lives in the Spring Hill Baths which were less than fifty metres from our house. Every day we crossed the street on which we lived, Boundary Street, ran the twenty metres to the International Hotel on the corner and turned right. About another twenty metres down Torrington Street was the pool—our own oasis of watery wonderment. We ran, not just because we were anxious to get to the pool but because we rarely wore shoes and our feet were burning on the road and footpath which baked in the sun.

The Spring Hill Baths boasted a twenty-five metre pool. It had an opening in the roof to let in the sun, which in turn heated the water, and with our Queensland summers, that did not take long. The pool itself was bordered by a narrow walk area with individual lockers along all four sides. At the deep end was a one-metre diving board, made of wood and covered in sisal matting. We played a game in which one of us would dive from the board while someone else took off from the side at the same time. The kid on the board had to dive straight ahead as fast as he could to avoid being caught. We might do that for hours and keep score of the number of hits or misses. From that diving board we also could execute expert one-and-a-half somersaults as well as a variety of full twists, half twists and swan dives, from the standing or running position. The diver always announced his or her choice of dive to an enthralled audience of three or four.

During the Christmas holidays, rain or shine, we went to the pool three times a day. We would spend the entire morning there, returning home for lunch. After lunch we were anxious to get back but Mum was a stickler for certain old wives' tales. 'You'll drown on a full stomach,' she said. And for some reason, if we ate watermelon at lunch time, there was to be no swimming whatsoever. What mystical element watermelon contained we could only imagine and Mum never bothered to explain.

'You have to wait at least an hour before you can go back into the pool.'

'Nothing will happen to us. We won't drown.'

'An hour.'

'Half an hour.'

'We'll see.'

Ten minutes later. 'Can we go now?'

'What did I tell you?'

And so it went until she reluctantly gave in. We would stay at the pool until about five, returning home for dinner, and then back for an evening dip.

It cost a penny each to get in so Mum had to fork

over fivepence each time. So—to do the maths—it cost her one shilling and threepence a day or eight shillings and ninepence a week. But if the manager of the pool was absent, we snuck in. Whether he noticed it or not, he never said anything.

We often had the pool to ourselves and nothing was more exciting than to arrive and see the water perfectly still, unrippled. The competition to 'break the glass' was fierce.

'We're the first! We're the only ones here!'

We hurled our towels into a locker and jumped in. The first thing each of us did was sink to the bottom and wait for the others. We held our breath and then, as each one got to the bottom, we formed a circle by joining hands. Who would be the first to break from the circle and head up for air? Everything we did was competitive, now that I think about it.

As time went on, it became apparent that my older brother Harold didn't need us as much as we seemed to need each other. He was the strongest and he enjoyed dominating us by dint of his strength. Harold always had to bat first at cricket, which was hard because we could never get him out. There was never any 'Well, that's enough for me. You blokes have a turn now.'

Harold had no hesitation in using his fists if we

crossed him or refused to do his bidding. It became easier to do what he wanted than risk a punch in the stomach or a push or a neck crusher. We were all afraid of Harold.

Harold was very close to Dad and he tried with all his being to please him. He knew that Dad loved football and boxing and cricket so that is what Harold focused on. He wanted to be the junior version of his father. They shared the same name, after all.

I was not close to Dad. It was instinctive. I wanted him to love me as much as he loved Harold, but it never seemed to happen. I never felt a great wave of love or affection from Dad, the way I felt it from Mum. Harold dominated Dad's attention. He enjoyed seeing a mini-version of himself. Strong, tough, assertive, brash. I was none of the above.

Our household was obsessed by sport. Our father was a man who believed that sports were a code of life. But no sport mattered as much as football—Rugby League. Playing football, watching it, listening to it, reading about it in the newspapers and especially talking about it were of primary importance in our house. My father was said to have been a good player as a young man, so good that he might have played for Australia if the Depression hadn't forced him to abandon any such plans and try to find a way to support himself. But that shadow of being 'good enough to play for Australia' was a long one and it hung over our heads all our young lives.

I remember one day when I was about twelve or thirteen. It was two weeks or so before Christmas. I announced to John, Ronald and Diane that I was going to swim the entire length of the pool underwater.

'No way, Tony,' Ronald said. 'Across and back maybe. But holding your breath for twenty-five metres? You can't do it.'

'I'll bet you I can!'

'I bet you can't,' John said.

'I bet he can,' Diane said.

'I'll bet you my mango I can do it!'

Every year around Christmas, our grandmother— Mum's mother—sent us a wooden case of mangos from Bowen in northern Queensland where she lived. Bowen mangos were the most delicious fruit we had ever eaten. Strawberry and yellow in colour, succulent and stringless, they were rationed out in a miserly fashion by Mum. Their sweet, tropical smell permeated the house. We ate them with the juice dripping down our forearms.

'You're on!' John said.

John thrust out his hand to seal the bet. I shook it and

then swished my hand lengthwise down his. He pulled back, not knowing what I was doing. I still held my hand out. He put his hand out again but this time, I slapped the back of his hand with the back of mine. He laughed and I laughed and then as if we both were thinking the same thing, we shook hands again. Once again, we shook hands, swished palms and then slapped the backs of our hands again only this time, we added to it. We placed our thumbs together and twirled them around in place so that our palms were now facing each other. We swished our palms together again. We both laughed, thinking ourselves very clever. We had invented a very cool handshake right there and then.

John walked away as I took my place at the shallow end, ready to dive in. I took several deep breaths. In I went.

Long, deep strokes were the best way so as not to exhaust one's air supply. We knew that from our games. The water felt good. I felt good. I could do this.

John, Ronald and Diane followed along the side of the pool. 'Go, Tony! Go!'

My eyes were straight ahead. The white side of the deep end of the pool loomed. It was getting harder and harder. My lungs were bursting, my head pounding. But I was not going to give up. I was going to make it. I could feel it. Three more long pulls with my arms and I should be there. Two...

And then I hit something. It was a foot. My head bolted back. It was like running into a wall.

I broke through the surface of the pool, gasping for air. I was a metre from the end. I shook the water from my eyes and saw Harold's tough, angry face glaring down at me. I was actually taller than my brother and had been for several years. But I was rail thin and Harold was much thicker set and naturally stronger because I had been sick a lot with the usual childhood illnesses of whooping cough and pneumonia which Harold never seemed to catch. But my height made no difference whatever when it came to who held the claim as being the toughest of us.

'We've got to go and see Dad,' Harold said.

'What did you do that for?' I asked him as I grabbed for the side of the pool. 'I was trying to swim a lap underwater!'

'Who cares? Get out of the pool. We have to go and see Dad.'

John was my ally. The one who went along with everything I ever wanted to do in a happy and supportive way. Being the middle child seemed to give him a sense of ease about himself. John said, 'We don't have to if we don't want to.'

Harold stood up. He pulled himself up to his full height and made a move towards John who backed away. 'You're all coming!'

The others looked at me as they always did at such times. I climbed out of the pool. 'We'd better do as he says. Dad must want to see us.'

Harold climbed out of the pool too and picked up his football.

'I don't want to go. I'll stay home with Mum,' Diane said. My little sister was totally adored and spoiled by us. There was nothing we wouldn't do for her and she returned the favour. She was one of the boys and was happy to be included in our games. She was very pretty, with a thick head of hair she usually wore in plaits which she hated because of the snarls that occurred after washing. I was putty in her hands most of the time.

'Mum's out shopping in town. You're coming with me.'

'Where are we going?' I asked.

'Where Dad's working today, stupid!'

We shuffled after Harold, made our way through to Boundary Street and headed south.

Diane was only five. It was a long way to walk and the heat made it worse. She looked to me with pleading eyes and it was only moments before she was on my back.

Spring Hill was a tough area. We were teased about it at school.

'You live in Spring Hill? With all the criminals?'

If you lived in Spring Hill you were poor. And we were no exception. But we always had whatever food and clothes we needed. Mum saw to that. She was a master of stretching a pound—and a penny for that matter.

Through the streets of Spring Hill we glumly trailed after Harold until we reached the wharf where several large cargo vessels were docked. Dad was a wharfie. The word bothered us, though Harold would never have admitted to such a thing—to his credit. I wished my father was anything but a wharfie. I wanted to be like everybody else—normal—or what I thought was normal. What Dad did for a living was not 'normal' for us. We didn't know the difference between snobbery and stupidity.

Wharfies were looked down upon by most Australians. Wharfies were the butt of many jokes at school. Wharfies seemed always to be on strike and news of these strikes was constantly on the front pages of the newspapers.

In the 1950s the Red Scare was alive and well. We went to Catholic schools. Wharfies were considered by many people, especially Catholics, to be communists because of their socialist-leaning union leaders. For a Catholic, wharfies were versions of the anti-Christ. But Dad was not a communist. He was a strong trade unionist but he always considered the communists, who were the most vocal members of the Waterside Workers' Union, to be foolish figures.

Some weeks Dad worked all the time, others not. It depended on the level of shipping traffic in and out of Brisbane. The amount of work Dad might get in a given week determined everything—food, clothing, the basics of life. If he got work, it was backbreaking—although, in time, he became a winch operator because his back just gave out. But some of the shifts went from midnight to 8 a.m. and, in winter, with the winds blowing over the river, it was unpleasant even in Brisbane's sub-tropical climate. And Dad hated the cold.

If he did not get work, he had a lot of time on his hands. Sitting around just gave him time to brood. He was not a person for hobbies though he flirted with gardening and for a time grew beautiful zinnias and dahlias. Whopping great blossoms, fantastic colours. Then he caught a fungus under his fingernails, blamed it on the fertiliser and gave it all up. So that left listening to and watching sports.

When we arrived at Dad's wharf at the end of Boundary Street, we watched as the winches carried the cargo from the wharf into the hold of the ship, guided by several workers. And then we heard the dreaded news.

'We're on strike, mates!' yelled a large man in dirty overalls. He was the foreman. 'All out!'

There was a sound of grinding metal. Engines and vehicles sputtered to a halt in an instant. Some of the pallets, suspended by ropes that carried the cargo, stopped in mid-air.

'Again,' John whispered to me. 'Oh, boy.'

'Dad probably knew it was coming and that's why he wanted to see us,' I said.

'Course he knew,' Harold said. 'That's why I brought the football—so we could go to the park and have some fun with Dad.'

'I'd rather be in the pool,' Ronald said.

'What will Mum do about food?' John asked me.

'You know Mum,' I said. 'She always has a few shillings stashed away.'

At least we weren't in school and subjected to the taunts of the other kids. 'The bloody wharfies are on strike again. Bloody commies!'

Then, from out of the hold, ascending like some otherworldly form from the bowels of the ship, Dad appeared, balanced athletically on a pallet. He rode the pallet towards the dock and jumped off. He waved when he saw us. His face was dirty but he stood tall and strong. He was a handsome man. A strong jaw, regular features, blue eyes and a full head of dark hair.

We all ran towards him.

'Hey, Dad,' Harold yelled.

chapter 2

Harold dropped back and indicated the football he held in his hands.

Expertly, with beautiful rhythm and style, he kicked the football to Dad who with even more grace and finesse caught it and swept it up into his arms. To make sure it was safe, he tugged it to himself, to show us—no, to show Harold—this was a sure way not to drop it or have it snatched from you in a game.

Still on the move from catching the ball and with no apparent change in step, Dad punted the ball high, high, high into the air. It was done with an extraordinarily fluid motion. No one could say that my father didn't know how to handle a football. Before he kicked it, he turned the ball so that the laces pointed upward. He held it at the correct angle and connected with it perfectly. It soared. We watched its arc in awe and admiration. Harold caught it.

Dad seemed to be in a good mood. We were happy that he was happy despite the fact that he was out of work and we knew that it would only be a matter of time before tensions over money would lead to unpleas-antness with Mum. Dad's moods were an essential barometer of our lives.

We walked with him to Victoria Park, a slight detour from our house.

'Tony almost swam the length of the baths under-water today, Dad,' John said.

'He would have if…' Ronald stopped in mid-sentence. The words died in his throat as he shot a hasty glance over at Harold.

'I'll do it tomorrow. I know I can do it now,' I said quickly.

Dad glanced at me and I saw in his face a puzzled look.

Would he say something?

'You kids are going to have water on the brain you're at that pool so much.'

We reached the park with its manicured fields. Harold immediately ran onto the grass.

'Catch this, Dad!'

Dad caught it and then signalled to me. I was positioned some distance from Harold, standing with the others.

He kicked the ball as effortlessly as ever. I saw it coming. Sailing high and then curving earthward. I prayed to every saint I knew to help me catch it. St Anthony, St Christopher, St Jude the Obscure. I sort of kept my eye on it. I sort of had my hands on it. I sort of pulled it back to my body, but it fell between my outstretched arms. I tried to anticipate its bounce but, swooping in like some fabulous bird of prey, Harold picked it up, hipped me to one side, ran a few steps and kicked it back to Dad.

I hated him.

John came over to me and we moved to the side of the field and sat down on the grass. 'Harold's like a pig in shit with Dad, isn't he?'

I nodded.

'Who cares anyway, Tony?' John said. He held out his hand. I looked at him and he smiled. I took his hand and then he swished his palm down mine and we did our handshake again. We laughed and it made me feel, for the moment at least, a little less hopeless.

The four of us sat on the side of the field and watched as Harold and Dad kicked the ball back and forth. But it was far too hot to be running around, and Dad begged off.

'I'm too old to play football in this heat,' Dad said. We began to follow him as he trudged out of the park.

Dad was in his early forties. My mother, Dora, was two years younger. Both were born and grew up in Brisbane. Dad's father and mother were from Ballythomas just outside Dublin. Mum's mother was born in Liverpool in England. Dad's father was a labourer. Mum never knew her father.

Both Mum and Dad had suffered in the Depression. They always spoke of it in the most sombre terms. Any conversation that began, 'During the Depression...' would be a forbidding tale of hardship and scarcity. It was a world for me that always existed in black and white. I grew to hate the word 'Depression' and was glad to have been too young to have experienced it.

Dad was not given to telling many stories about when he was young but I learned enough to know that he had a tough childhood. He was alone for much of his youth because his mother would abandon him on occasion and place him in an orphanage. She drank. Dad's father was either dead or gone—we never quite knew for sure because I never once heard Dad refer to him. And so Dad shuttled back and forth between the orphanage and whatever home his mother would make for herself and him. He also spent a lot of time sitting outside hotels waiting for her.

When the Depression hit, like thousands upon thousands of others, Dad took to the road to fend for himself. He headed to wherever he thought he might find food and shelter and it was not oftentimes found in the cities. It took its toll on him in many ways, the significance of which I wouldn't grasp until many years later.

The War signalled the end of the Depression but that didn't mean the end of deprivation. One sign of this was the ration books we used during the War and for a time afterwards. Whenever I ran errands to the nearby grocery store to get things for Mum, I always had to take the ration books which Mum kept in a Bushells tea tin on top of the kitchen cabinet.

But after the War, there was mass immigration. Australians were being introduced to a more cosmopolitan world which would reshape their identity. A whole new era was beginning, in which I would come of age as well, even though our family's outlook on the world and in particular our Australian world was insular and tough.

I had always longed to travel. American soldiers had been stationed not far from our house during the War. In fact, Douglas MacArthur's base camp in Brisbane was in Victoria Park, where we went to kick the footy. America, therefore, loomed large in my young life and, because America helped save Australia from 'those Jap bastards' as Dad called them, we loved anything American. I wondered what it must be like to live in a country as big and as powerful as America, so far across the seas. The Hollywood movies made America seem limitless in size and possibilities.

On our way home from the park we passed the Spring Hill Baths. Diane was back on my shoulders. 'Now I can see what's going on, Tony,' she used to tell me.

As we passed the International Hotel, the distinctive smell of beer mixed with heavy-duty floor cleaning fluid wafted out the window. We knew that smell well.

An old friend of Dad's stuck his head out a side window. His name was Tommy Thurman and he was Dad's oldest and closest friend. Dad didn't have many close friends but Tommy had grown up with Dad and had travelled with him during some of his days in the bush during the Depression. Tommy was one of the few people who ever visited us at our house. It was a ritual that he came every Sunday night and he was always a most welcome guest as far as us children were concerned. He had been married but his wife had died and he had no children. He never arrived empty handed. He always brought us each a Hoadley's Violet Crumble bar which we all devoured down to the last chocolatey smear and crumb of honeycomb. For Mum, he would bring half a dozen crabs—mud crabs if they were in season—for Sunday night dinner.

'G'day, Harold,' Tommy said.

'G'day, Tommy. Bloody hot day. We're on strike again.'

'Yeah, I heard, Harold. Going to be a long one, do you think?'

'Who the bloody hell knows? These bloodsucking ship-owners are killers, that's for sure. They don't care how I'm going to feed my kids.'

Tommy also worked on the wharves, sometimes with Dad. 'I'd invite you in for a drink,' Tommy said, 'but I know you won't.'

'Yeah, mate. You know the old saying: one's too many and a hundred's not enough.'

Dad never drank. We all knew that he had once been a heavy drinker but Mum had exacted a promise from him that he had to give it up if they were to marry and have children. Dad was evangelical on the subject. He despised people who drank too much. He had no tolerance for those he witnessed staggering out of the International Hotel. There was never any liquor of any kind in our house.

Diane slid down from my shoulders. She turned to Ronald.

'I'm going to be the first to see Mum,' Diane said.

'No, you won't. I'll beat you.'

Harold, John and I waited with Dad as he chatted with Tommy Thurman. Tommy's drinking was not a sore subject with Dad because we never saw Tommy drunk and I don't believe he was a very heavy drinker—certainly not the kind who stayed at the pub until he couldn't walk. He was a widower and sought the company of other men. Dad knew that and understood it.

I watched as Ronald caught up with Diane. I decided to leave the talk of strikes and ship-owners. I nodded at John. He nodded back at me and we walked together across the street to our house.

chapter 3

Dad rented our house which, like many in Brisbane, was built on stilts to take advantage of the cooling summer breezes. This provided us with a wonderful area under the house where we played marbles, had a swing and raced our toy cars. We had a front verandah with a rocking chair which looked out over the railing at the street and the passing parade below. We loved to stand behind Mum or Dad and rock them and look out. Mum once told me that when we were little, all under ten, she would sometimes have us all around her on the rocking chair—for an afternoon nap. She would be holding Diane, maybe breastfeeding her; Ronald would also be on her lap; the other three of us would sleep either leaning up against her legs or hanging off the rocking chair.

The house was square in shape and divided in two by a hallway. At the front was the verandah which had blinds above the railings. These helped keep out the sun and rain but were almost always pulled up. Once inside the house, there was Mum and Dad's bedroom off to the right which was comfortably big with a small alcove where the newest baby slept. As Diane grew up, this alcove became hers. I don't know how Mum and Dad retained any privacy for themselves as she grew older but there just was not room for Diane to have her own bedroom.

John, Ronald and I slept in the room opposite, roughly the same size as Mum and Dad's. Further down the hall towards the back end of the house was another bedroom, where Harold slept. Why he was given this room to himself was never questioned. His bedroom faced the lounge which doubled as a dining room. The dining-room table had matching chairs, and the sofa and overstuffed chairs were a 'set'. It was called a 'Genoa' set. Mum had bought it all on time-payment. The dining table was in the centre of the room and the sofas and chairs placed around the walls. We ate at the dining table only on festive occasions or when we might have visitors. We usually ate at the large table in the kitchen. The living room also contained an upright piano. Diane and I were the ones who chose to take piano lessons. The living room was dominated by a large standing wireless.

Just past the living room was the kitchen and back verandah. The kitchen was large enough for a table which seated the seven of us comfortably. We had an ice-chest which required the daily delivery of a block of ice. Remarkably, it kept things cool. The kitchen also contained a sink with a tap but no hot water and a stove which was set into a chimney. Off the back verandah was the bathroom which contained a sink and a bath. The toilet (the lav) was down the back stairs in a dwelling unto itself. Our house was sewered but many people living in the suburbs in Brisbane had lavatories out in the backyard. Some people planted flower beds around theirs or even grew creeping vines over them. But there each one stood, in all its glory, in full view of one's neighbours who knew when you went and how long you might spend in its dingy interior. Because the waste was not flushed away, one doused it with a generous helping of sawdust conveniently placed in a built-in box next to the throne itself. The sawdust box was kept filled each week by the men who came to replace the tins. These were the dunny men. We were extremely sympathetic to the job they had to perform.

So, even though our toilet was not inside the house, it was at least sewered. Diane was deathly afraid of spiders in the toilet. Our toilet was not lit, ensuring that night-time forays to it were kept brief and to the point. At the finale, we used newspaper torn into square pieces which were hung in a hessian bag nailed to the inside of the door. Toilet paper was a luxury unknown to us for many years.

There were other luxuries we did without. We had no running hot water. Baths required water to be boiled. Fortunately, with Brisbane's warm weather, this never seemed to be a problem. Mum boiled water on the stove and brought that to the tub. Then the landlord installed a gas water-heating system. This hot water only provided us with baths, not showers. To rinse soap from your hair, which you always washed first, you knelt before the spout from the water-heating system and allowed the water to run through it. You had to light the pilot with a match and then swing it inside the heater itself. The pilot lit the ring of jets, which, in turn, heated the water. It made an ominous whooshing sound. I lived in dread of it, fearing that one day it would explode through the roof like the little spaceship (which it greatly resembled) that blasted off from Krypton and brought the baby Superman to Planet Earth and into the lives of Mr and Mrs Kent of Smallville.

The radio in our living room, in those days before television, was as important a piece of furniture in our lives as anything we owned. The news was never to be interrupted with noise from any of us. Any violation of this could send Dad into a tirade of anger. Neither was there to be any noise during the cricket matches which droned on for days or the weekly football matches, which were doubly sacrosanct.

Our favourite programs were 'Inner Sanctum' which opened and ended with the sound effect of a creaking door. Its grisly stories were terrifying to us because we imagined them so vividly. By the end of the program, we were riveted to our chairs, unable to move. We loved 'The Hit Parade' on Sunday night. We kept the lists of the shifts in popularity from week to week of songs like 'Vaya Con Dios', 'Good Night, Irene' and (God help us) 'How Much Is That Doggie In The Window?' Our favourite late afternoon serials were 'The Search For The Golden Boomerang' (with its introductory music from Tchaikovsky's 'Nutcracker'), 'Superman' and 'Biggles' which was about a flying ace named Bigglesworth and his group of brave friends who battled everyone from the

Nazis to bank robbers. Biggles always gave chase in his plane, no matter the locale. This never seemed to us to stretch credulity. 'Biggles' also was never, but never, to be missed.

On Sunday nights, the entire family and Tommy Thurman always listened to 'Take It From Here' which starred Dick Bentley and June Whitfield. They were Ron and Eth, an ordinary English couple. Our imaginations ran right along with the words and sound effects. Despite its being English (and Dad detested anything English) 'Take It From Here' made him laugh. We marvelled that he didn't seem to mind Ron and Eth's Cockney accents. Normally, he needed to hear only two or three words spoken in an English accent on the radio to declare, 'Turn that Pommie garbage off!'

There was another program I remember though we never listened to it because it came on in mid-afternoon while we were in school. We only knew about it because it was Mum's favourite. If we happened to be home sick or it was a holiday, we heard parts of it. It was really a soap opera so we didn't have the slightest bit of interest in it. It was called 'When A Girl Marries'. It had the best, corniest lead-in I've ever heard, delivered by an announcer with a sonorous voice of plush velvet. It went like this: '"When A Girl Marries"…For all those who are in love and for all those who can remember...'

Then there was the birthday call program. 'And a special cheerio call to Henry who is celebrating his seventh birthday today. I understand he is having a party today with all his friends. Mother and Father send all their love as well as Aunt Betty and Uncle Bert and cousins, Larry and Dorothy. And you'll find a very special present hidden behind the sofa in the living room.' Imagine having anyone other than your immediate family to your birthday party! We couldn't. I think parents had to write to the radio station to have their kid's name read out. I ached to have my name read out. The thrill to hear one's name on the radio! I loved to run to the radio and turn it on and listen to the cheerio calls on my birthday—just in case. But mine was never called.

We had a large backyard, big enough to be able to approximate the length of a cricket pitch and we used it that way in the summer months. This would become our football field in the winter. If we needed to spread out or play with friends, we went to Victoria Park. I once decided that we needed a flat surface in our backyard so that we could hit tennis balls up against the brick chimney. Together, John, Ronald, Diane and I levelled the ground and were able to practise our backhands and forehands thereafter.

In running around the yard, however, we always had to be mindful of the clothesline held up by props, a piece of wood with a V at the top. The clothesline stretched the length of the yard and ball games were forbidden that day if Mum had a wash drying.

Washing day for Mum was a production. Her laundry set-up consisted of two stone sinks at the rear of the house where a cold water tap was attached next to the chimney and beside the back stairs. There was a large copper cauldron heated by firewood (and later gas) to boil the clothes in soapy water. Mum stirred the clothes in the cauldron with an old broom handle. Then she would haul them into one of the sinks to be rinsed in water in which hard chunks of bright blue bleach, wrapped in a piece of cloth, had been dissolved. The clothes were finally rinsed in starched water. Everything was spotless. Perfectly clean clothes and her impeccable ironing were Mum's pride and joy. And what a lot of ironing! For a husband and four boys and a girl—mountains of it.

When Ronald and Diane got home, Mum was in the middle of her laundry chores. I saw them run to her and touch her apron more or less at the same time before they ran off again. She had finished her shopping and come home to the grind of the weekly wash. From where I stood with John under the house, she seemed to be enveloped in a cloud of steam. She must have spilt some water onto the flames and the hiss of steam all but shrouded her. How hot it must have been for her standing over that cauldron! I could see her close friend Billie Moore was beside her.

Billie was everything Mum was not. Mum was a tall woman, about five feet eight inches in the old measure. She fashioned her hair in the style that Greer Garson popularised in *Mrs Miniver*—a part down the middle and curled up on the sides. By the time she'd had all five children, she was overweight. Billie was tiny, about five feet tall. We always thought she was the absolute pinnacle of refinement. She lived two doors down from us on Boundary Street in a flat above the shop on the corner. Attached to the flat were two large rooms which housed her dress-making company. She had as many as a dozen women cutting and sewing dresses. That fact alone made her unusual in our world—a woman boss of her own company. Mum had worked as a seamstress before she was married and had quit as soon as Harold was born. Mum and Billie were great friends. We didn't have a telephone but Billie would often stop in and see Mum. She always found a way to make Mum laugh and admired her for her strength and the way she dealt with all five of us. And Dad.

Billie dyed her hair blonde, wore make-up and high, high heels, and smoked. She dressed in the latest fashion, usually in outfits she had designed herself in her factory. Mum had at most four dresses—two of them for good 'dress-up' occasions, which were few. Billie had two dogs and she drove her own car, a new Ford with fins at the back that made it look more like a luxury liner. The flat she shared with her husband, Peter, was decorated in a stylish 'new' manner. I remember it being mostly white on white with many knick-knacks set on tables and always with several vases of fresh flowers scattered around. We thought it was like something out of a magazine.

Peter was a gentle, kind Englishman who also took a great interest in us all. He was very tall—over six feet three—so he and Billie made an odd pair when they were seen together. Mum once told us that Billie and Peter were actually not married at all. They seemed to us terribly sophisticated.

John and I looked at each other nervously. 'Hello, Billie,' we said, more or less in unison.

'Hello, you two boys,' she said. 'I was just giving your mother this material. We had an over-run at the factory.' Billie held out a half bolt of a green tartan material. She turned back to Mum. 'Oh, by the way, Dora, I heard on the wireless that the wharfies are on strike again.'

'I know. I heard it too,' Mum said.

From the cauldron, Mum extracted a pair of Dad's heavy dark work overalls. 'I won't be washing these rotten things again for a while, I suppose.' She dropped them back into the boiling water. 'I don't know what's worse with all these strikes. Having no money coming in or having Harold home all day long.'

Billie handed Mum the material.

'Oh, Billie. You're too kind. It's lovely,' Mum said. 'There's enough here for shirts for all the boys and a dress for Diane.'

'Dora, I was hoping you might make a dress for yourself?'

Mum gave Billie a 'You don't seem to understand what priorities are' look.

'Dad's coming,' I said quickly.

Dad was in a good mood and we were all determined to keep it that way if we could. He didn't like people in the house. He didn't even like it when our cousins came to play with us. With any of Mum's friends, he was rude and insulting. She chose the wiser course and saw people when Dad was not at home.

'I guess we don't have time for a cuppa after all, Dora,' Billie said. 'I'm off.'

She knew the score as well as we did. It was not that

she was afraid of Dad. She did not want Mum to be subjected to his anger.

She turned to John and me. 'Heaven forbid your mother should have a friend to talk to.' She headed towards the back stairs to go under the house and out the front gate.

'Billie…' Mum said.

Billie turned.

'The material—it's lovely. There might be enough there for a skirt for me. I'll see.'

'I know. Come have a cuppa with me when you can sneak out. I'll show you the new designs I've been working on.'

As Billie reached the back stairs, Dad and Harold came out from under the house.

'Hello, Harold,' Billie said. 'Hot weather.'

'Yeah.'

Billie threw a little wave back over her shoulder to Mum and went under the house and was gone.

Mum turned to the pushbasket which stood near the clothesline and pegged out the few remaining articles of clothing. Once done, she hefted the forked pole that held up the line into the air. The clothesline was jammed with clothes along its entire length.

As she headed towards the back stairs, she passed

Dad and Harold who sat there. 'Another strike?'

'Looks like it could be a long one. You going to manage on what you've got saved up?'

'And if I can't?'

'You'll have to.'

chapter 4

We followed Mum and Dad inside the house. When we got to our lounge room, Dad was already collapsed on the sofa.

'Well?' Mum said to him.

'Well, what?'

'You know what today is?'

'Yeah, I know. Our anniversary. I thought with the strike coming…'

'Oh, no,' she said. 'That's not good enough. You have to give me something. We've been married fifteen years today.'

Dad started to say something but, for once, nothing

seemed to come. What was she driving at?

'Okay, okay. I'll make it easy on you. Remember the first time you took me out?'

'Aw, turn it up, Dora,' he said. 'I don't know what you're talking about.'

'What is it, Mum?' Ronald asked.

By this time, all five of us had gathered in the living room. In turn we sat ourselves in the various chairs. Diane jumped into my lap.

'It's something your Irish grandmother taught him. He knows.'

'Is it a card trick or something?' John asked.

'No, it's not a card trick,' Mum said gently.

'Come on, Dad,' I said. 'Please?'

'You'd like me to make a mug of myself in front of my own kids?' Dad said with a half smile.

'You won't make a mug of yourself. Go on.'

Diane jumped off my lap and ran to Dad. 'I love card tricks, Dad.'

And then Dad started to sing.

'When Irish eyes are smiling,
Sure 'tis like a morn in spring,
With the lilt of Irish laughter
You can hear the angels sing...

When Irish eyes are happy
All the world seems bright and gay,
But when Irish eyes are smiling,
Sure they'll steal your heart away.'

As Dad sang the second verse, he was beginning to feel slightly uncomfortable. Apart from his singing, you could hear a pin drop. His voice was beautiful. We had never before heard him use it in song. We were riveted. We had never seen anything like this before.

I looked across at Mum. She had an ever so slight smile on her lips.

He was about to go into the third verse but stumbled for the lyrics. Mum stood up. 'Okay, okay. That's enough,' she said. 'I'll put you out of your misery.'

There was a moment of silence.

'Sing it again, Dad,' I said.

'That was really bonzer, Dad,' John said.

'No, that's enough. He doesn't have to do any more. I just wanted to see if he remembered.'

Dad stood and headed for the kitchen. 'Oh, I remember, all right.'

Mum followed him towards the kitchen. 'I suppose you'd like a cup of tea after that, Mr Bing Crosby.'

As they left the room she reached out and ran her

fingers up the middle of his back and squeezed the nape of his neck. This was not usually how our house was—or at least how Mum and Dad were with each other. I never once saw Dad kiss Mum or vice versa—not even a peck on the cheek when he came home from work.

Dad was moody, unpredictable, opinionated and quick-tempered. His abuse was most often directed against my mother but we were not excluded. Dad felt that he could say whatever he wanted, wherever he cared to and whenever he felt like it. He had no discipline about his feelings. He simply didn't care. There was no warning, no hesitation, no apology. What strangers or even friends thought about such moments was of no interest to him.

Not long after this, Dad took John, Ronald and me into town by trolley bus, to buy us our new clothes for the school year. Ronald was a robust little squirt and always into mischief. When he was about six or seven, he was hit by a car in front of our house, though he wasn't hurt. Because of this incident, and because he was always on the move, we always considered Ronald some-what accident prone. Ronald was the last of us to get on the bus and somehow managed to get only halfway in as the doors closed on his head. As the bus took off, and before the driver could stop, Ronald was running along beside it, his head caught in the door.

Dad shouted at the bus driver to stop. 'Jesus Christ! Stop the bus, you stupid mongrel bastard! You've caught my kid's head in the bloody door! You stupid imbecile! Stop the bus!'

The bus screeched to a halt and Ronald suffered no serious injury except perhaps to his pride.

We occasionally went to the movies with Mum and Dad on Saturday nights. I remember we went to see Greta Garbo in *Camille*. Mum wanted very much to see it. We were making our way up the aisle of the cinema after the beauty and power of Garbo's death scene. Many other patrons, like Mum, were wiping the tears from their eyes. Mum sniffed, 'Have you ever seen anybody so beautiful? I hated that she had to die.'

'You would like that, wouldn't you, you stupid bitch?' Dad said in a loud voice so everyone around us could hear. 'Why did I let you bring a man to rubbish like this?'

Dad's 'dark silences' were often with us. At such times he would eat meals alone after we had had ours. We had to remain quiet in case undue noise upset him even more. Those silences could last for days—a week was not uncommon—and could come and go with no apparent provocation. We had no idea what he was thinking. We were so relieved when he would be out of his room and smiling and talking to us all again. It seemed at times that our lives alternated between his rages—violent and abusive—and his silences—cold and deadly threatening.

I remember most days I would walk home from school wondering what kind of mood Dad would be in, hoping, praying he would have a cheery 'Hello, son,' when I came in. He took out all his frustrations and anger on Mum. It was always her fault when he hit his finger with a hammer or misplaced something. If she protested, it provoked him all the more. Sometimes she refused to sit back and take abuse for something for which she was blameless. She would fight back.

We would urge Mum to walk away, to ignore the barbs he would fling at her. But she would hold her ground, even provoke him. An argument would start between them and there would be a full-scale shouting match. We would all cringe at the cursing and the name-calling and, when that had subsided, the silences would resume for days at a time again.

This is why I always remember that amazing day when I swam the length of the Spring Hill pool, the day Dad went on strike and he sang 'When Irish Eyes Are Smiling'.

Dad only hit Mum once. One Sunday morning, he stayed in bed. Mum tried to ignore his frostiness as though nothing was in the least unusual. She cooked a big breakfast for us as she did every Sunday morning—bacon, eggs, toast, tea. Since he was clearly not joining us in the kitchen, she decided to bring his breakfast to him on a tray. She went to the bedroom and said, 'I've brought you your breakfast in bed, Harold.'

'Shove your breakfast up your fat arse,' he said.

'No, no,' she said evenly. 'That would be a terrible waste of perfectly good food. But if that's the way you feel,' she went on, 'here it is!' She tossed the whole tray at him, turned and walked away. He was covered in food and liquid.

'Christ, you filthy cow,' he yelled. He bounded from the bed, screaming abuse. He slipped on the fried eggs—or the bits that were not already splattered over him and his pyjamas—picked himself up and caught her. She stood there, oddly amused at what she had done.

'Ooh-ah,' she said. Then she began to laugh.

'Think it's funny, do you, you bitch?' He whacked out at her but she ducked and he didn't quite connect. He slipped again and Mum decided that discretion was indeed the better part of valour. She ran from the bedroom and down the hallway towards the front door of the house. The five of us in the kitchen, now alerted to the tumult, were hot in pursuit to protect her. Harold jumped Dad from behind and rode him as if he were a wild bronco.

'Don't hit her,' we were all yelling. 'Leave her alone!'

Then Dad stopped. There he was at the top of the stairs, a fourteen-year-old kid dangling from his back, the others pulling at him and trying to stand between himself and Mum. He looked a fright. He started to laugh. 'Maybe I will have some breakfast after all,' he said. 'Bacon and eggs would be nice.'

He went back to his room, dressed, cleaned up the mess and re-appeared as if nothing untoward had ever happened.

Violent arguments were not the only events that took place in our house. There were many happy times. Dad, in his rare expansive moods, had a slashing sense of humour.

He was an exponent of rhyming slang. 'It's a bit young and old today' he'd say, meaning 'It's cold today' or 'How's my dinner plate?' meaning 'How's my mate?' He used many such expressions with ease, dotting his conversations with them. We pretended we remembered their meanings, even if we did not always. There was one odd but colourful expression both Mum and Dad used which I never quite figured out—'Oats for goats, horses for courses and tin hats for wooden heads'.

It had something to do with accepting things as they are, I think.

Our father worried about money all his life. He was the youngest of seven. His father died when he was eight. Only two of his sisters and one brother survived to grow into adulthood. He loved his surviving sisters and hated his older brother. But who took care of them when they were young? Were they left to fend for themselves as well? We were never told. And we never asked.

He never once said his mother was wrong to abandon him at age ten and put him in the orphanage because she could not cope. 'It was the times,' he said. 'They were tough.' In fact, I never heard him say anything hateful or deprecating about her. He was like a lot of Irish men who had a peculiar obsession about their mothers. So often, Irish mothers were pictured as sweet, adoring, grey-haired Madonnas with hand-knitted shawls wrapped around bent and slender shoulders. They were long-suffering, knowing, tolerant and sainted. It was this image, this ideal, to which their wives had to aspire.

All Mum ever said about her mother-in-law was, 'She was a horror!'

None of us ever knew her. She died when I was three.

Up until I was about ten, Dad made Harold and me

go with him to the cemetery to his mother's grave a couple of times each year, and always on Mothers' Day. Her grave was high up on a hill and a long way from the gate of the cemetery. It was a cheerless place. Once we arrived at the grave itself, we found it covered in several months' worth of weeds. We had to pull them out and clean off the sad glass flower display encased in an upside-down glass bowl. Then one of us went down the hill to fill the single vase with water and place the flowers we had brought with us in it. There was no sign of Dad's father's grave. I never thought to ask where he might be. Once her grave looked as nice as we could make it, Dad would ask us to say a prayer and then we'd leave. Then, one year, Dad decided he didn't want to go any more, which pleased me no end. It was a hot, dreary business.

What was that hold his mother had over him? Why did she give him up? The drink was the obvious reason. I remember Mum saying that she used to cadge drinks in the ladies' bars of hotels. She was a lush. With her own husband dead and her other children able to fend for themselves, the decision was made. Let the priests and nuns take care of her youngest son when she didn't want him and then, racked with guilt, see him occasionally and spoil him.

The orphanage became home to my father. Stern

people ran those kinds of places. The cruelty he was subjected to left scars. He hardly ever talked about the orphanage, but when he did he was always vague. He talked about it differently from other things in his younger life. He always seemed sure of himself when he discussed something but that was not the case with the orphanage. What happened there?

At any rate, he ran away from the orphanage when he was thirteen. He was on his own from then on.

chapter 5

The peace didn't last long. We could feel the tensions growing minute by minute, hour by hour. Dad was home all day, the strike might drag on and the pressure of paying for the groceries at the store made him edgy all the time. And Christmas was around the corner.

Dad listened to the cricket all day long. Just sitting by the radio. Mum coped with the household chores with no help from him.

When Mum and Dad were first married, he worked as a house painter. He still stored his brushes under the house. They were always carefully cleaned and dried so that the bristles remained soft and pliable. We were never allowed to use them or so much as touch them.

Mum had a plan. 'I've spoken to Mick Moore on Wedd Street, Harold. He needs his house painted.'

'So why doesn't he do it?'

'He can't do it. He's working. He needs a professional and you've got all those paintbrushes under the house. It could take a couple of weeks. A good chance to make some money. I told him you'd be happy to do the job.'

'*You* told him! Jesus Christ, Dora! I'm not going to work while I'm on strike!'

'Why on earth not? We could certainly use the money!'

'You'd like that, wouldn't you? You'd like me to scab on my mates.'

We heard this conversation from where we sat in our bedrooms. It took place soon after breakfast and before we planned to head for the pool. It was a morning we decided to go a little later because John had just received a new supply of comic books which he had traded with several other kids in the neighbourhood—Superman, Batman and Robin, Archie and Jughead.

'If what your mates think is more important than feeding your kids...'

'You're the one who wanted five bloody kids. I didn't. You find a way to feed the little bastards! I'm on strike!'

'And are you going to be the one to ask the grocer for credit?'

'Bugger the grocer!'

We were already in our bathing suits and halfway down the front stairs. The angry voices behind us were fading.

'Keep your voice down! The neighbours will hear you.'

'You think I give a shit about what the neighbours think?'

We raced across the street, passed the pub and headed to our haven.

'I'll be first in today.'

'No, I'm going to be.'

'No, me.'

My brother Harold wandered in about half an hour later. He signalled to me. I got out of the pool and went to him. He was dressed in his football shorts and shirt as he most usually was and had obviously been playing football or some game with his mates because his knees were grass-stained and his clothes were dirty.

'There're some kids outside who are making fun of the wharfies. Rotten bastards. I'm going to bash them up. Come and help me. Go and get John.'

'Ah…I don't think so, Harold.'

'What are you talking about? They called Dad a commo.'

'That's nothing new. I'm not getting into any fight and John isn't either.'

Harold glared at me. 'You're nothing but a rotten little sissy. You don't want to get hurt, do you? Think you might get a bloody nose or something, little goodie-goodie?'

'I'm not going to go out there and fight some kid over what he said about the wharfies. I don't care what they say and I don't care what you say.'

'Poofter!' He walked away and out of the pool area.

When we got home, Harold was nursing a cut on his lip and his eye was swollen and would most likely be black the next day. He stood at the head of the stairs as John, Ronald, Diane and I walked meekly through the front gate.

Dad's head appeared. We stopped in our tracks at the foot of the stairs.

'You rotten little curs. You couldn't help your brother with those louts who called your own father a commo?'

'I didn't want to get into a fight,' I said. 'I didn't see them or talk to them. Harold did and he wanted to fight them.'

'One of those kids was really big, Dad,' John said.

'All the more reason you should have stuck together and helped your brother.'

'Mum told us that she doesn't want us getting into fights,' I said. I regretted it the moment it was out of my mouth.

'You little poofter!' Dad said. 'Hide behind your mother's skirt, that's right. You were always a little dingo bastard. Get out of my sight!'

Harold smirked. I stood at the bottom of the stairs looking up at them both. I turned and headed under the house and sat on the swing we had there. Slowly, the other three joined me and sat on the ground, saying nothing.

There was never any question that I was closer to Mum than to Dad. I was the 'soft' one. Coming so soon after Harold who took it upon himself to be the mirror image of Dad was a hard act to follow. It wasn't that I, in turn, leaned on Mum. It was probably the other way around. In an effort to compensate for what she saw as Dad's allegiance to Harold she went the other way. Harold was 'Dad's boy' and I was 'Mum's boy'.

I loved my mother. She was kind and warm and funny and generous. But, most importantly, she was a good person. She loved people too much to hurt anyone. The more Dad retreated from people, the more she gravitated to them. What an odd pairing they were.

My mother lived for her children. She gave us every-thing she had. 'Your kids, your kids, your kids,' Dad used to say to her. It was a kind of anthem in our house. We were her job, her charity, her hobby. We were what she got up in the morning for.

Mum came from an even stranger family than Dad did. The only grandparent we ever knew was Mum's mother—we called her Gran. We were always a little afraid of her. Sometimes it was hard to believe that she was Mum's mother. She was a harsh, vindictive, humour-less creature and I loathed her. And she didn't care much for me either. Nor did Gran particularly care for John or Ronald and, what with Diane being a girl, well, she simply did not count. Harold, she loved.

There was never any mention of a grandfather, Gran's husband. We were told he was dead. Much later, when I was about nineteen, Mum received a letter in the mail from a man telling her that he wanted to see her. In the letter—which Mum was very secretive about—the man said he was living in Brisbane. He urged Mum to come and visit him. 'He wants to talk to me about giving me some money,' she said.

'But who is this person?' I asked.

'Someone who knew your grandmother.'

I imagined the letter-writer was a long-lost relative, an avuncular type who had appeared on the scene like something out of Dickens and was going to bestow good fortune on this favoured stranger—my mother. Perhaps he remembered the time she had helped him across the street one day or had done some small kindness like giving him a bowl of soup during the Depression.

Mum was unable to resist the call and went off to meet her correspondent. I drove the budding heiress to meet him that night. I was told to wait outside in the car. Mum was with him for about an hour. When she returned, she said simply, 'Let's go home.'

'How was it? Who is he?'

Mum refused to answer.

'Who is he?' I pressed.

'He's my father, Tony! Now, that's enough and I don't want to discuss anything more about it.'

We drove home in silence.

Although as far as I know Mum saw him many times after that, we never laid eyes on him. We did learn that his name was Jack Battersill. In later years, I resented terribly his intrusion into my mother's life for what I considered his own peculiar and selfish reasons. When he died, he left his money to a sister.

Mum openly confessed that she never wanted her

time as mother to her chicks to end. She wanted her children always to be her children, and she wanted to be able to give us whatever we needed.

One of the things she decided early on while I was at convent school and being taught by the Sisters of Mercy was that I should learn to play the piano. She must have had an uphill fight of it with Dad, but I liked music and I took to playing the piano and became quite good at it. I loved to play the works of Beethoven, Mozart and, my favourite, Chopin.

Not long after the incident on the front stairs, I was practising the piano and playing Chopin's 'Minute Waltz'. It was one of our whole family's favourite pieces (including Dad's). It's a wonderful piece for the piano with lots of frills and a joyful melodic line. Perhaps it was the family favourite because of its title—we all assumed that it had to be played in a minute, which would have been completely in keeping with the competitive spirit of our household. My fingers would race through those notes like a bat out of hell. I remember using a stopwatch to record how quickly I could play it. But I never managed to play it in a minute.

Harold stood at the side of the piano as I played.

'We're playing cricket in the backyard. We need you to bowl.'

I nodded but did not take my eye off the keyboard.

'I'm playing this now. Mum wanted to hear it.'

A moment passed and then the piano lid was slammed down hard on my fingers. I jumped off the piano stool and howled in pain.

'You do what I want, or else!'

I stood up, pushing the piano stool back. I clutched my fingers and faced him. A hard right in the stomach stopped me from making another move.

I bent over in pain. Harold turned and walked out of the living room and headed towards the back door. Holding my stomach, I followed behind him. As I reached the back verandah, I was still holding my stomach and fighting back the tears. It would do no good for Dad to see me crying about something like that.

Mum appeared from out of the kitchen where she was doing her ironing. 'Why have you stopped playing?' she asked.

'I can't. Harold slammed the lid down on my fingers.'

'Harold!' Mum said to Dad who was standing at the railing looking out at the backyard.

'And he punched me in the stomach because he wants me to play cricket with him.' I was telling tales but who cared at this point? It happened all the time so it was hardly news.

Dad turned to face me. 'Did you punch him back?'

'No.'

'Well, do it! Use your fists on him.'

'But I can't...'

'Harold, that son of yours is nothing but a horrible little bully. He's always pushing these younger ones around.'

Dad said nothing and walked inside the house.

'It's all right, Mum. I'll go and play cricket. It's not worth having Harold getting mad at the other kids.' I went down the back stairs and took the cricket ball from Ronald.

I heard Mum's voice as she followed Dad inside the house. 'You've got to do something with that son of yours. He's only doing things like that to please you and it's not fair to the others.'

I bowled the ball to Harold who hit it over the fence. John chased it down in the tall grass of the neighbour's yard and we played for over an hour, in a vain attempt to get Harold out.

Shortly after this, Mum was in town shopping when we arrived home from the pool for lunch.

'Tony! Come here!' It was Dad's voice.

I made my way under the house and out to the back-yard where he was. There to one side was a boxing ring.

Dad had found some rope from somewhere and had cordoned off a square area with it. There were four poles that he had pounded into the ground to approximate the corners. It even had two small stools in diagonal corners, and draped over those corners were two pieces of rag. One red, one blue. Seated in the blue corner was Harold, wearing a pair of boxing gloves. Where had those come from?

'You're going to learn how to box, son. Put these on.'

I looked at Harold. He was smiling at me and made a motion across his nose with the thumb of the gloves, the way boxers do to indicate they're ready for battle.

I looked at John and pushed my hands into the gloves. Dad tied the laces. He moved me to the red corner and sat me on the stool. The gloves felt like they weighed a ton.

'All right, there's no bell so come out to the middle and shake hands,' Dad said as he picked up the two stools and placed them outside the ring.

To the middle of the ring we went and touched gloves.

Dad separated us and then stepped back.

Harold immediately took a boxing stance and it looked as if he had done so all his life. I tried to follow suit but I was not certain which hand to put up to my face. I didn't have time to consider this for more than a moment because from nowhere came a blow to my face that almost knocked me to the ground. My head bolted back and I was stung with how much it hurt.

'Keep your left up to your face,' Dad said.

Whack! Another stinging blow hit my glove which in turn hit my face. My head lashed back again.

'Move around. Move around. Circle him. Circle him.' This advice was meant for us both. I started to move in the direction opposite to the one Harold was moving in.

'How about this, Dad?' Harold said and immediately dealt me a blow to my stomach.

'Good, son. Another one. One two, the way I showed you.'

Harold shot a left to my body and a right to my face with blinding speed. I didn't see either of them coming and the one to my nose connected hard and brought tears to my eyes.

If I knew one thing I knew I must not cry. I swallowed hard.

Another sharp blow to my head. I reeled back.

'What the bloody hell's wrong with you?' Dad said. 'What do you think the gloves are for? Hit him!'

'I'm trying! I'm trying!' I started forward, swinging wildly with both hands. I didn't care how it looked.

Harold dodged my flailing arms and, just for good measure, hit me in the stomach.

'That was good. Now another one.'

I stopped what I was attempting to do. It was futile. I stood still, breathing hard. I faced Harold squarely. I put my gloves to my face and wiped my nose, now flowing freely. Then the worst happened. I felt tears rolling down my cheeks.

'What the hell are you crying for?' Dad said.

'I'm not crying,' I said.

'Yes, you are. Tony's crying. Mummy's little boy Tony is crying!'

'I am *not*!'

'Fight like a man!' Dad said. 'You're nothing but a rotten little sissy. You can't fight any better than you can catch a football. Jesus, how could a man get a son like you?'

'Come on, little sissy. Little piano player.'

Harold did a duck-and-weave motion which looked something like what a professional boxer might do. I could only sway more or less, as it were, in reflection of him.

'Good, Harold. A left to the head. A right to the kidneys.'

Harold obeyed. I felt more hurt than physical pain. I

was in that ring with two opponents. I was fighting my father as well.

Behind me, I could hear Diane crying.

I found something. The tears were flowing freely now and the snot. I held my right hand to my face and charged at Harold with all the strength that was in my body. I charged and hit blow after blow. I was hitting as hard as I could. I got hit back but I didn't care.

From under the house, I heard a voice. It was Mum. She was in a full run. 'Stop! Stop! What on earth is going on? What are you doing?'

I stopped and looked around to see her. Her arms were filled with Christmas packages which she tossed onto the back stairs. She came to the ring and stood there glaring hard at Dad.

'Are you out of your mind?' she said.

Mum made her way into the ring and came to me and pulled my head to her body.

'You want the kid to grow up to be a sissy? He's got to learn how to defend himself.'

'Don't do a thing like this again, Harold.'

Mum took my hands and yanked at the laces, undoing them. Once she got the gloves off, she threw them to the ground and pushed me ahead of herself, putting my head between the ropes and out of the ring.

'You're always sticking up for him. You're ruining him.'

Mum did not look back at Dad and moved to the stairs to gather her packages. I too moved to the stairs and plopped down. John came and sat beside me, saying nothing. I was breathing hard and sniffling and wiping the tears away from my face. I felt John's arm go around my shoulder. Ronald and Diane came over and stood mutely in front of me.

Back in the ring, Harold began bouncing around, throwing fake punches, shadow-boxing, doing all the moves that boxers do in the ring. He hit out at Dad who, taken by surprise, turned and faced his oldest son. Dad put up his hands in a perfect boxing stance and began to dance around him. He hit out at Harold but he didn't hit him. After a few moments of this, he placed his right hand on Harold's head to stop him.

'That's enough for today, son.'

He took Harold's hand and raised it high in the air, the way a referee might do. Winner and champ!

chapter 6

A day or two later, the strike ended and Dad was back at work again. Christmas and the summer holidays rolled by and soon we were back at school.

Our class had a football game every week. I was on the green team; the other team was red. Dad had an afternoon off from work and I was told that he and Mum wanted to come and see me play. I tried to discourage them.

'What, are you ashamed of having your schoolmates see your parents?'

'Of course not. I just don't think it will be all that good a game. We're the Bs. I'm not on the A team. No one's particularly good on our teams.'

'We'll be there at two to see you play.'

'Please, please, if the ball comes to me, please don't let me drop it,' I prayed to St Anthony, St Christopher and anyone else who might be listening. 'I'll help old ladies across the street, I'll never say an unkind word again in my life, I promise to go to Mass on a weekday and say an extra rosary tonight. Just, please…'

Dad sat on the sidelines watching like a hawk. I knew that unless I scored all the tries and made spectacular tackles, it would be a disaster. It came as no surprise that I hardly got the ball and when I did I fumbled it badly. Not only did I fumble it but as I was running forward, bent over, my right foot kicked the ball, sending it even further away from me. Bad as this was, it was made all the worse by the fact that had I only been able to pick the ball up cleanly and hold onto it the way Dad had taught us all to do, I might have scored because I had no one in front of me and the goal line was wide open.

I didn't dare look across at the sidelines at Mum and Dad. I could imagine the smoke coming out of his ears.

On the walk home, Mum tried to keep up a genial chatter but Dad wore a stony face and said nothing.

When we got to our house, Harold, John and Ronald were sitting on the front stairs waiting for us.

'G'day, Tony,' Ronald said cheerily. 'Did you score any points in your game?

I could see Mum trying to hush Ronald but it was too late.

'Yeah, for the other team maybe,' Harold snorted.

I walked past them quietly into the house, followed by Mum and Dad. The others entered the house too and followed me down the hallway towards the kitchen.

Things have a way of going downhill at a galloping pace when the fates decide to conspire against you. This was not my day. I reached for the loaf of bread that was sitting on the table. A slice of fresh bread, some butter and a little jam would taste good. I picked up the bread knife and looked to see which type of jam I might like. Thus distracted, I managed to knock the loaf of bread to the floor. I froze. I could feel Dad's presence behind me.

'Jesus Christ. Look at the kid. Just like trying to catch the bloody football. Completely bloody hopeless.'

Mum and John and Ronald were there now. They heard what Dad said.

'He did his best, Harold,' Mum said. 'We can't all be great footballers.

'It's all your fault! Pushing all this piano playing. Pushing them all to become bloody sheilas!'

I stood, rooted to the spot, not even daring to

pick up the loaf of bread at my feet.

John stepped forward, picked it up and placed it back on the kitchen table. 'Dad, we've been waiting for Tony to get home so we could all go swimming. Why don't you come swimming with us?'

'I don't like swimming, son. You know that.'

'But can't you just come and watch us? You never come and watch us.'

'Nah. You kids go by yourselves. You can take care of yourselves.'

I found my voice. 'It would be fun if you came and watched us swim, Dad. We could show you…'

I didn't get a chance to finish. I wanted to tell him about the new dive John was able to do—with my help. We'd been practising. If I ran behind him on the diving board, step for step and jumped when he did and landed on the board at the same time, I could give him more spring and he could go higher into the air. He was able to do a double somersault that way. When John did the same for me, I wasn't able to get completely around for a full two somersaults but I would eventually. John was just naturally good at anything involving the water.

'Fancy yourself as Esther Williams, do you?'

We loved Esther Williams movies. She was an enormous MGM star in the days of the great studio system—the Julia Roberts of the 1950s except that all her movies featured big choreographed scenes in swimming pools. Whenever one of her movies came to the Metro theatre, I bundled the younger three together and off we went. I doubt we missed one of her films. We even went home from the theatre and tried to imitate some of her balletic movements under the water in the Spring Hill pool.

'Go on, Harold,' Mum said. 'You've got nothing better to do. Watch the kids play.'

'Make me a cup of tea first.'

We were all at the pool by the time Dad wandered in. He never liked to swim. Hated the beach and stayed out of the sun if at all possible. For a sports lover, he had a surprising dislike for a lot of outdoor activities. He chatted for a while with the pool owner and then took a stool from the man's office and sat on it behind the deep end.

I was at the shallow end with Diane and Ronald. One of the games we liked to play a lot was swimming through each other's legs. Two or three of us would stand in a line with our legs open and the one whose turn it was would swim through the tunnel of legs without touching. Sometimes, we'd close them and clamp on tight just for the fun of it—usually with Diane. She would come up squealing and protesting but loving the fun. Distractedly, I looked down the pool towards Dad, trying to get into his thoughts. Trying to understand what made him the kind of man he was.

Dad had an odd way of sitting at certain times. He had long thin legs and would cross them at the knees and around the ankles. It was strange to see. He looked around the pool and waved at John who had yelled at him when he saw him. If he'd hung a sign around his neck which read 'I am utterly bored and I'd rather be anywhere but here', he couldn't have been more obvious about his baby-sitting chore.

We moved from one game to another. The memory of my dismal showing at football was dimming just a little. I picked up a penny and tossed it some distance from where I stood. Like a porpoise, I dived forwards to find it. I retrieved it quickly and swam to the surface. I threw it again but this time not so far. I wanted to try to catch it on its zigzaggy path before it hit the bottom of the pool.

When I came up for air and swam to the side of the pool, Harold was there. 'I didn't bring a coin with me. Give me yours.'

'No,' I said. 'Get your own. Or go outside and get a rock or something.'

'Give it to me or I'll take it.'

'If you want it, you're going to have to take it from me,' I said.

I tossed the coin as far as I could towards the deep end, pushed off and swam as fast as I could go.

Harold gave chase but it was no contest. I even took a look back and I thought to myself, 'I could be at the deep end, get out, see the coin on the bottom of the pool, dive for it, pick it up, get back to the surface and even have enough time to read the novels of all three Brontë sisters before Harold could catch up to me.'

I swam as hard as I could. I got to the deep end and pulled myself up out of the pool. I could see my coin on the bottom of the pool and was about to dive back in to retrieve it when I saw Dad stand up from his stool and walk towards me. He had a look on his face that I had never seen before. He had his finger pointing at me and his mouth was a little slack.

'Where did you learn to swim like that?'

'Like…like what?'

'Like what! Like *that*! What you just did, for Christ's sake.'

'Here.' Wasn't it obvious?

'Do you always swim as well as that?' Dad said.

'I guess so. Have you seen John swim? He's faster

than me at freestyle.'

By this time Harold had reached us but, seeing Dad talking to me, simply looked up at us both and listened.

Dad called over to John. 'Swim over here to me, son.'

'Okay, Dad,' John cheerily replied.

He pushed off and swam leisurely over to us. From as far back as I can remember when we first learned to swim, John was a natural. He looked absolutely beautiful in the water. Everything was flawless about his stroke and his kick and his breathing.

Dad said, 'Line up here and swim to the end of the pool when I say "Go".'

John and I stood side by side, looking at each other in befuddlement.

'I'm not going to swim anywhere,' put in Harold.

'Who asked you?' Dad said.

Harold looked as if he had been slapped hard in the face. He got up and headed for the exit.

Dad took no notice. 'To the far end, as fast as you can go. Ready...Go!'

We dived in and swam for all we were worth to the shallow end. Dad walked the length of the pool, never taking his eyes off us. John finished a moment ahead of me, which wasn't unusual. Though we never raced, when we were chasing each other he was always that little bit faster. It didn't mean anything. He just was.

'Can you do that again?'

'Sure, Dad,' John said. 'Watch Tony do backstroke this time.' John turned to me. 'Show Dad how you can do backstroke, Tony.'

I nodded.

'Go!'

We did. As fast as we could. When we got to the deep end, Dad was there. Backstroke is not as fast a stroke as freestyle so John finished a second or so ahead of me. I swam backstroke a lot during our games. On my back, I could see everything, where my brothers and Diane were at any given time.

'Bloody hell,' Dad said as we touched the other end again. 'Bloody hell!' He looked around as if he wanted to shout the news to someone. Anyone. 'We're going to show these mugs a thing or two.'

He started to walk away towards the entrance of the pool, leaving us standing in the shallow end, baffled. He called back over his shoulder. 'Be back here at five and we'll start training.'

'Dad,' I said as tentatively as I could. 'I've got a piano lesson at five today.'

'Not any more you don't. We're about to do something serious here.'

71

I looked across at John. He looked at me and shrugged his shoulders.

'Bloody hell!' Dad said as he left the pool area shaking his head.

After that, our lives were never the same.

part 2

TONY, RONALD, JOHN 1956

chapter 7

The next morning we were hustled out of our beds.

'Rise and shine,' Dad said as he walked from bed to bed, pulling covers off us. 'Up you get!'

It was still dark. I sat up wondering what awful thing could have happened at this hour of the day.

'What is it? What's wrong?'

'It's ten to six. Time to get up.'

John groaned. Ronald, who was sitting up in his bed, fell back and pulled the covers over his head.

'The pool opens at six. We'll be there to see it open.'

Dad left the room and I leaned over to John. 'What have we got ourselves into?' I whispered.

'It's hardly light out,' John said.

'It's all your fault for swimming so well yesterday,' I said accusingly.

'You started it when you swam away from Harold.'

'I don't like the look of this at all.'

Dad was back in the room. 'What did I tell you? Do you want me to drag you out of bed? Get up! Now!'

We hit the floor, scrambled to find some clothes and were out of there in less than two minutes. Sure enough, the pool gate was opening as we came down Torrington Street.

I can't imagine how Dad knew what it took to train for swimming, given that he knew precious little about the sport. But it seemed that overnight he worked out how to train us to be competitive swimmers. He had a plan. And we would live by the rigorous rules of that plan for years.

Dad drew up our training schedules. The number of laps and at what pace. As we got closer to competition, we swam sprints to get us sharp.

We were immediately signed up to join the major swimming club in Brisbane, the Valley Club. Club meetings were held every Wednesday night at the Valley Pool in Fortitude Valley. This pool was fifty metres long and ten lanes across. I remember the first time we went there.

The lights played on the beautiful aqua water and there were ropes running down it to mark off the lanes. We were bug-eyed.

Dad signed us up for a series of races in our age groups. I was entered in the freestyle and backstroke events and John and Ronald in the freestyle. It was a circus, with parents jostling to sign their kids up while two men wrote their names in a book.

In my first race, I swam fifty metres backstroke in the under-thirteen age group. I won easily. I was very pleased with myself.

John was extraordinarily talented. At ten he could beat anyone in his age group by several seconds—a big margin in swimming. He could also beat the best of the other swimmers in the club several years older than himself.

After his first race in which he beat the competition by at least five metres over fifty metres, Dad took it all very much in his stride.

'I must say you don't seem terribly pleased by John's win, Harold,' Mum said. 'I thought you'd be thrilled.'

'This is nothing,' he said. 'The state championships are coming up. We'll show these bastards a thing or two then.'

A bond developed between Dad and John. It grew

with every passing week as John's times dropped by seconds. They chatted together a lot after training sessions. It was not so much that I was excluded, just that John talked easily with Dad where I did not. Nothing much changed in our relationship. I knew that now our family's hopes were resting on John's shoulders and that was a mighty responsibility. I know John felt it—he told me so. He also knew that he could not, dare not, let Dad down.

Before each race, a routine was firmly established between John and me. We always did a quick version of our handshake to wish each other good luck. We knew it was a little silly but it was our personal connection and it meant a lot to us both.

My brother Harold was completely left out as the obsession with swimming consumed our world. It made him bitter, defensive and unhappy. He went from being the favoured one to the one who was barely tolerated. He had little choice but to fend for himself and grab what little attention from our father was left over.

The months went by and we kept getting faster. In January 1954, at the Queensland State Championships, I won the Under-Fourteen Queensland Backstroke Championship. It was thrilling. Even Dad seemed pleased.

John was entered in the Under-Twelve Freestyle. He won by over two seconds and set a new Queensland record for that age group. He was immediately heralded as the fastest young swimmer in Australia.

A ritual began right after John won that first title. When he touched the wall, so far ahead of the competition, Dad stood in his place and began to cheer. 'You little beauty!' he yelled. 'You little beeyootie!' He could not stop himself. Hundreds of people turned to look at him, and began to laugh. Perhaps they thought it was genuinely funny. He was so excited, so happy that John had won. A proud father. But we hated it. For years after that, after every race we won, it became a mantra for him.

'You little beauty!'

I once made the mistake of going to Dad before one of my events. 'Please,' I said in as conciliatory a tone as I could. 'If I win, don't yell "You little beauty!", okay?'

I'll never forget the look I received. He was stunned, but only for the barest moment.

'You little poofter,' he spat at me as I shrank from him. 'I'll yell whatever I want to.'

We asked Mum if she could intercede and do something about this 'chant'.

'It isn't so much that your father wants to draw attention to himself,' she said. 'What he's trying to do is to rub your swimming success in the noses of everyone there.'

We sat on one side of the pool and the 'fancier' crowd sat on the other. The kids who sat on the other side all had paid coaches and their parents were in reasonably successful professions. The swimmers usually sat with their coaches and the others who were in their training squad.

We were not part of a squad. We were coached by Dad and so we just had each other. It was not so much that he coached us on how to improve our stroke in the water. He didn't know anything about that. We came by that naturally. He was more like a trainer, setting a regimen for us to follow each week, making sure we stuck to it—every metre of it. He started us off with the longer distances early in the season to build up our stamina. Then we did the same number of laps but broken up into shorter distances. As we got closer to an important race, we did mostly sprint work. This same routine was repeated in the afternoon. His regimen was strict and we dared not shirk from it for fear of incurring his wrath. It was not a lot of fun but we knew no better. At the peak of our training, we would have swum as much as eight kilometres a day.

The pools opened on the first of September. And

that's when we started our season each year in preparation for our state championships. For the first month or so, the water in the pool was freezing. It made no difference to Dad. We had to be up at five-thirty, rain or shine. Even the man who opened the pool for us went back to bed after he let us in.

The calm surface of the pool—once something we'd competed with each other to be the first to break—had lost its appeal. We dreaded it—one toe in and then a shiver, hugging ourselves around the chest. John would look at me and I at him, both knowing that deep in our hearts we wished we could be anywhere but there— preferably in bed. Dad would tolerate our hesitation for no more than five minutes. Then he would get up from his seat and walk over to us. With steely eyes, he'd say, 'Get in.'

'It's so cold today, Dad…'

'You think I'm going to waste my time watching you little sissies stand there and look at the water? Get in, I said!'

'If we don't train this morning,' John once said, 'we promise we'll do double this afternoon when it's a bit warmer, won't we, Tony?' I nodded in agreement.

'You won't,' Dad said. 'You may be able to fool me by not doing your training but you can never fool yourselves. Get in!'

At that point, if we didn't, he simply pushed us in. We would take a deep breath, and break the surface of that cold, cold water and stop, gasping for the air that had been shocked out of us. We would swim for almost a lap with our heads above water gasping until our bodies became accustomed to the temperature of the pool. On many mornings, we would have terrible headaches at the end of our workout but it was useless to complain.

I hated September.

Dad, to my knowledge, never once went into the pool. I'm not even sure if he could swim.

chapter 8

John won the same Queensland Under-Twelve Freestyle Championship three years in a row, setting new records each year, breaking his own records in each instance.

He was the undisputed star of the family. He was very famous in Queensland. His picture was in the newspapers often and once a story appeared about him in the national sports magazine, *Sporting Life*. Dad became so used to seeing John's picture in the paper that, if an article appeared about any other young swimmer, it would upset him.

'Fancy showing a picture of a kid like that! Kid can't swim. He won't go anywhere! Didn't they hear about

John's swim last week in the club championships?'

Dad started a scrapbook and religiously cut out any mention of us in the newspapers, even the small print of the actual race result and times. He took John into town and had his portrait taken in a photographic studio. The black and white photograph was enlarged to five feet by four feet and placed in an attractive frame. When Dad brought it home for us all to see, he already had the spot selected where it was to go. In the centre of one wall in our living room so that it dominated the entire room.

Mum took one look. 'Do you think it's big enough, Harold?' she said wryly. 'I mean, I feel I should light a candle in front of it or something.'

Dad bristled slightly at this but said nothing because nothing and no one could deprive him of the fact that in time…in time…

Large numbers of trophies, silver cups, small and large, silver plates and dishes, glass bowls, decorative spoons and trays were arrayed around the room. We won everything. Dad bought a very handsome china cabinet to house some of them. The biggest trophy we had looked like a smaller version of the Davis Cup. I won it for several years in a row. It was called the Morrell Cup, named after the man who served as chief starter at all our club meets and the Queensland and

Australian championships. It was given to the most outstanding swimmers for the club each year and was voted on by the officers of the club so it was considered a high honour. And like the Davis Cup, it had to be returned at the end of each year, unless one won it again, of course, which either John or I did. Dad was extremely pleased. He never did much work around the house in terms of helping clean or dust or even make beds but those cups were always clean! That was his job. And they sparkled.

It was hard on Harold. When he turned fourteen, he refused to go on to high school. Mum and Dad simply should never have allowed it; but at any rate it was decided that he must have a trade. Harold became an apprentice bricklayer. It was a tough job but he took to it and there was no shortage of work. Brisbane was growing in leaps and bounds. Houses, schools and offices were springing up in new suburbs.

The rest of us were determined that we would have a secondary education. The only problem was—how to pay for it. We had all attended a Christian Brothers School called St James which was at the bottom of Boundary Street—a fifteen-minute walk from our house. But it took boys only up through the eighth grade. We wanted to go to St Joseph's College, Gregory Terrace.

This was the premier Catholic boys' school in Brisbane. It was a large school with about seven or eight hundred boys enrolled in primary and secondary level. Each class had about thirty-five boys in it and the teachers were Christian Brothers. It faced Victoria Park and was close to our house. It had the reputation—and we were all intensely aware of it at the time—of being a snooty school. You only went there if your parents could afford to send you. Sons of doctors, lawyers and businessmen sent their boys to Gregory Terrace (as it was generally called).

Dad played his trump card. He and Mum went to see Brother Adams, the head of Gregory Terrace.

'Come right in, Mr and Mrs Fingleton,' he said. 'I've been expecting you but you'll have to forgive me. I forgot that today is the feast day of St Thomas Aquinas and Father Mahoney is here to celebrate Mass for us.'

'Oh, well, we'll wait or come back,' Dad said.

'Unless you'd like to come and hear Mass with us,' Brother Adams said.

'No, that's all right. Why don't we come back tomorrow or whenever it's convenient for you?'

'No, please.' Brother Adams seemed now strangely insistent and Dad, for once playing the ever-reasonable man, got the hint.

'Yes, why not?'

'Indeed. Why not?' It was as if he was trying to outdo Dad in being obsequious.

Brother Adams led Mum and Dad to the chapel on the third floor of the main building. It was a beautiful chapel with stained-glass windows and prie dieux instead of pews. There was an aroma of incense. The small altar was always bedecked with huge vases of flowers.

Brother Adams pointed to two prie dieux next to his and knelt down. Mum and Dad took their places. The Mass had already started. Brother Adams opened his missal and joined in with the liturgy. At a lull in the proceedings, Brother Adams leaned towards Dad. 'You wanted to talk to me,' he whispered.

'We have three boys, Brother.'

'I know who they are. *Et cum spiritu tuo*,' Brother Adams said loudly. Then in a whisper, 'They are wonderful swimmers, your boys.'

'I want them to come to this school. It's the best school in Brisbane.'

'I see,' Brother Adams said.

'But I can't afford to send them here.'

'*In nomine Patris et Filii et Spiritus Sancti.*'

Dad's Irish Catholic mother would most certainly have made him go to church when he was a young person. Mum was Church of England but she never went to church as far as I can recall, although it was she who pushed us to go to Mass every Sunday and obey all the teachings of the Church. Dad cursed at the whole business of it. And, of course, he hated the Pope. A stupid bloody Italian bastard!

They made a curious combination. One parent not Catholic, driving her children to live the Catholic experience and the other, the Catholic, violently opposing the Church and its teachings and not giving a hoot whether or not we were 'pure and god-like and in a perpetual state of grace'.

'*Et cum spiritu tuo*,' intoned Brother Adams. He fell to his knees. Mum and Dad followed suit, a moment or two behind.

'You want to win the inter-school swimming championships this year?' Dad whispered across to the prie dieux next to him.

Brother Adams nodded.

'And the year after that?'

Brother Adams nodded again.

'Take my kids. John's the best swimmer his age in Australia.'

'And Tony is state champion,' Mum chimed in.

'*Pax vobiscum.*'

When Mass ended, Brother Adams led Mum and Dad from the chapel.

'Oh, Mr Fingleton, if you're lucky, Father Mahoney can hear your confession. He's staying on for an early lunch. He'd be only too happy...'

'That's nice.'

'It's probably been a while...'

'A little while, yeah.'

'But he'd love to go to confession, I'm sure,' Mum said. 'Wouldn't you, Harold?'

'I'll do it next week.'

'Since you're here and since the boys are coming to our school...'

Dad's face lit up.

'With no tuition fees, though?'

'Who mentioned fees?' Brother Adams took Dad by the arm. 'Father Mahoney is right this way.'

'Bloody hot in here, isn't it?' Dad whispered to Mum.

'Not for us Protestants,' Mum said.

Dad made the most of it. 'I hope this Father Mahoney bloke's got plenty of time...'

'Oh, I doubt there's anything Father Mahoney hasn't heard, Harold. May I call you Harold?'

chapter 9

A few months later, Dad was on strike again. He had gone to Hamilton Wharf—one of the bigger wharves along the Brisbane River—to join a large group of workers to protest for better pay.

As John and I walked home from training, we chatted about the strike. Would there be more fights? How would Mum make ends meet? And the Australian Championships were coming up again. Would any Queensland swimmer win a gold medal?

'I can't wait for the time when you and I are on the Australian team together, Tony. Won't that be something? The two of us wearing Australian blazers?'

Harold and the Fingleton kids. From left, Harold Jnr (Kain O'Keeffe), Ronald (Robert Quinn), Diane (Keeara Byrnes), John (Thomas Davidson), Harold Snr (Geoffrey Rush), Tony (Mitchell Dellevergin)

Harold Jnr, Harold Snr, Tony

Above: the Fingleton family. Clockwise from top left, Tony (Jesse Spencer), Harold Jnr (David Hoflin), Ronald (Craig Horner), Harold Snr, Dora (Judy Davis), Diane (Brittany Byrnes), John (Tim Draxl)

Left: Billie (Deborah Kennedy) and Dora

Training at the Spring Hill Baths

The North Sydney Olympic Pool—Harold gives John some pre-race instructions

A heart to heart for Tony and Dora

Tony (Jesse Spencer) at the Empire Games, 1962

Swimmers of Tony Fingleton's era with cast members at the Valley Pool, Brisbane. From left, *standing* Michael Wenden, Kevin Berry, Murray Rose, John Konrads, Geoffrey Rush, Tony Fingleton; *seated* Ilsa Konrads, Dawn Fraser; *kneeling* Remi Broadway (as Murray Rose), Tim Draxl, Jesse Spencer, Melissa Thomas (as Dawn Fraser); *front* director Russell Mulcahy

'Imagine being the best in Australia at something,' I said.

'You know the best part?' John said. 'When we win, Dad's happier and he and Mum don't seem to have as many fights. Have you noticed that?'

We came to the International Hotel, then turned the corner from Torrington Street into Boundary Street.

That evening had turned stormy. Dad was still out with the striking workers. Thunder clapped and lightning made our radio crackle. It was a delicate instrument at the best of times and this kind of weather brought out its temperamental side. We were listening to our evening programs because our homework was done. Mum was mending some shirts of Dad's in one of the chairs near the radio.

Then there was a loud thump and we all jumped. Was that the radio? No, there was the noise again. Was it the wind knocking something down on the front verandah? Then, again. A crashing noise this time followed by a voice, but it wasn't saying anything. It was more like a groan.

We all sat straight up. Mum was the first to move. She'd been tense all evening. She must have suspected something was up. She was already halfway down the hallway before any of us could react.

I moved quickly to catch up to her and, just then, there was another flash of lightning. Standing in the doorway was a figure. The lightning threw everything into sharp focus. A very eerie sight, almost cinematic. Another flash of lightning revealed the shape of the figure in silhouette. It looked like Dad. It was Dad! He was weaving and holding tight to the sides of the front door.

'He's been in an accident,' I thought. 'My God, he's probably bleeding somewhere.'

He made another noise, a sort of snuffle. We reached the verandah and Mum turned on the light switch. The others had all by this time reached the verandah.

Dad looked completely different. His clothes were soaked and he clutched two soggy paper bags. His face seemed somehow contorted as if he were having trouble breathing. His eyes opened and closed but stayed closed longer than they stayed open.

'Oh, dear God.' Mum was the first to speak.

'What is it? What's happened?' I asked.

Just then, one of the paper bags gave way and a bottle fell to the floor of the verandah and rolled towards us. It was Castlemaine XXXX, a brand as familiar to us as Coca-Cola. We watched the beer bottle roll. I felt I was somehow outside myself, a bystander in all this. But there was no mistake. I was there.

Dad took a step towards Mum but teetered as if he might topple backwards down the steps. Harold grabbed him by his upper body and steered him towards a chair. Dad collapsed heavily into it. He still hadn't uttered a single word. Harold crouched beside him.

Diane tugged at my arm. 'What is it, Tony? Is Dad sick? Has he been hurt?' She started to cry.

A loud clap of thunder.

Ronald asked, 'What is it, Dad? Are you sick?'

'He's drunk, you little idiots!' Harold barked. 'Can't you see that?'

'She'll be right, mate. She'll be sweet,' Dad said at last. He handed the wet paper bags to Harold. 'Put these in the fridge for me, champ.'

Harold took them, got up and went past us.

Mum moved to Dad and stood over him, one hand to her head and the other on her hip. 'Why have you done this, Harold?'

Diane was now crying uncontrollably. She was tugging at my hand. I looked down and saw her tears.

'He's going to be all right. Stop crying now.'

I knelt beside her and held her tight. I looked across at Dad. He had made a move to get out of the chair but fell clumsily back into it. John and Ronald moved quickly to him and helped him stand.

'There are my two mates. How are you, son?' he said to John. 'You little beauty.' He smiled at John who looked back at him, unsure whether to smile or cry.

'Bring him into the kitchen,' Mum said.

Mum hastened inside and stepped quickly into her bedroom as John and Ronald helped Dad down the hallway. Harold had by now returned and took Ronald's place alongside Dad.

'I've got him,' Harold said.

I tapped John and Ronald on the shoulders. 'You two take Diane to our room and read to her while I help Mum.'

They nodded and veered off into our room. I waited long enough to see them put Diane in my bed and then made my way out to the kitchen.

By the time I got there, Dad was using a tea-towel to dry his hair without much success. Mum came with Dad's dressing gown. She took the towel from him, took his shirt off and wiped his chest. Then she draped the gown over his shoulders. Harold had, by this time, opened one of the bottles of beer and was pouring some into a glass which he then set on the table.

Dad looked up at me.

'Hello, son,' he said warmly and smiled.

'Hello, Dad,' I said. I smiled back at him.

'When I was as old as you,' he said, 'I was older.'

I hadn't a clue what this meant. I just nodded. Then I realised that it meant that by the age of fourteen, Dad had had much more experience of life than I had. 'I know, Dad. I haven't done much.'

He took a large swig from the glass. I was astonished to see that he drank almost the entire glass in one swallow as if he were desperately thirsty. But how could he be? Clearly he had been drinking for hours. This registered very strongly because it gave the impression that he was completely in the thrall of the beer—the way he swallowed it so greedily. The beer seemed to consume him rather than the other way around. He handed the glass back to Harold for a refill. By this time Mum had managed to dry him off, more or less, with the towel. She had taken his wet pants off him, wrapped the dressing gown around him and tied the sash.

As he put the glass back down on the table, he looked over to me again.

'Dad, I don't know why you've done this. What's wrong?'

Then he started to sing, never taking his eyes off me. '*When Irish eyes are smiling*,' he sang. '*All the world seems bright and gay, With the lilt...*' He picked up the glass and looked at its amber contents as if it were a magic potion of some kind. 'I'd been on the road all by myself.'

Another swig from the glass, draining it this time.

'I know. It must have been pretty hard for you.'

'What would you know? Why don't you come over here and sit on me?'

The skin crawled on the back of my neck.

Mum shot to her feet and bolted towards me. 'Go to bed, Tony! At once!'

'Wha...?'

Mum started pushing me backwards into the hallway. 'What did Dad just say?'

'Just go to your room. I'll be with you in a minute.'

She turned from me and went back into the kitchen. It was dawning on me that Dad wanted to hurt me as much as he could at that moment. 'This is what he really thinks of me,' I thought. 'He really hates me to say something like that, knowing how hurt I would be.' I wanted to cry but I was too shocked. I stood there, within earshot, unable to go to my room and unable to turn back to the kitchen.

I heard Mum's voice. 'How could you, you vile thing?'

'You don't know what a kid like me had to do just to survive in the Depression.'

'You are despicable, Harold. I've never heard anything so ugly in my life. You can say what you like to me and God knows you have. I'm used to it. Tony's never done anything to hurt you in his entire life.'

'*You can hear the angels sing...*' He seemed now to be taunting her. 'I had to do anything I could. Rotten bastards. There were a lot of rotten bastards out there on the road. What he made me do. For a few lousy bob so I wouldn't starve. Rotten panno now.'

He was rambling now and I couldn't take hearing his voice any longer. I staggered towards my room and went in.

I vaguely heard Mum. 'But Tony had nothing to do with that. Why did you say that? How could you?'

'I had to eat.'

John, Ronald and Diane all looked up to me as I entered the room. They were in their beds and Diane was in mine. 'Is everything going to be all right, Tony?' John asked.

'I don't know. I don't think so. Diane, why don't you sleep in here with me tonight?' She nodded. I turned to John and Ronald. 'I just want to go to sleep.'

I felt bereft and filled with sadness.

I heard Diane's steady breathing and knew she was asleep. I heard strains of 'When Irish Eyes Are Smiling' coming intermittently from the kitchen and Mum pleading with Dad to be quiet.

About half an hour later, I heard Mum come into the room. She sat on the side of my bed and touched my shoulder. I didn't move. I pretended that I was asleep. She tapped me gently again.

'Tony?' she whispered.

Nothing.

I felt her get up off my side of my bed. She pulled the covers over my shoulders and smoothed down my hair. Through a slit in my eyes, I saw her pat Diane's head and then she went out. I heard her head towards the kitchen.

chapter 10

I was always a very good sleeper—that was the first night I knew what it was like to toss and turn. When I got up, I stirred John and Ronald awake and we quietly went about our morning ritual, which is to say, we got our bathing suits and towels and sneaked out of the house.

When we got home around eight o'clock, Mum was up. She was in the kitchen, sitting by herself, her chin cupped in one hand, nursing a cup of tea. She smiled as we all walked in. 'Would you like some breakfast?'

'We're happy with cereal, Mum,' John said.

'You know where everything is.' She didn't budge

from the table. She gave me a look that was unutterably sad, and nodded her head slightly. I nodded back. And then I went down the back stairs.

I had been planting tomatoes, beans, some lettuce and carrots in the back garden. I sat on my haunches and pulled out a few weeds.

Mum approached. I didn't look up. 'I know it must be hard for you, darling,' she said. 'I can't undo it. What's said, is said. You know I love you. That should count for a lot.'

'Is this drinking going to happen again?' I pulled a carrot from the ground, wiped the dirt from it and rinsed it under the hose. I bit into its sweetness.

'Darling, I don't even want to think about it. If it's anything like what he used to do before you were born, we're in for something. He was a heavy, heavy drinker. I made him give it up when we got married but now that he's back on it again, I just don't know what to think.'

'Mum, Dad doesn't care about me, does he? I mean, sometimes I feel he doesn't even…like me.'

'No!' She knelt down beside me and held my face in her hands and turned me to look at her.

She bit on her lip. 'Sometimes, these things happen and they happen for a reason. This is going to make you strong, no, stronger! It must! Don't let this throw you. I know you feel awful about what your father said last night. But…'

She too pulled a carrot from the ground and wiped away the dirt from it. She rinsed it under the hose and then sat down on the grass beside me and began eating it.

'Your father's a very difficult person. Maybe it has something to do with his mother. You never knew her and believe me you missed nothing. She was an awful drunk. Your poor father was on the streets half the time.'

'But that doesn't explain why he does the things he does and says the things he says. I can't help that his life was so terrible. I don't know why I'm such a disappointment to him. There's more to me than not being good at football and boxing.'

'Of course there is. He knows that. It's simply that…'

Mum said nothing for the longest moment. She looked away and sighed. Then she turned back to me.

'I don't know why he said what he said. It was cruel and it was rotten. I think he was trying to lash out and hurt someone. It's usually me. You have to try to forget what he said. You know, your father did some pretty awful things to survive in the Depression. He hates himself for it.'

'But what has that got to do with me?'

She got up and took the hose in her hands and began to water our little garden.

'Are you as strong as I think you are?'

'Not as strong as Harold.'

'I don't mean physically.' She tapped her forefinger to the side of her head. 'Up here. That's where you have to be strong. You can beat your father. You can beat Harold. Keep going and never look back on all this. Show your father what you're made of.'

I was not convinced and she knew it.

'I think you have a right to know what I am about to tell you. Something happened to him yesterday. Something quite awful.'

'Besides getting rotten drunk?'

'It's what made him go to the pub.'

She turned off the hose and sat down again beside me on the grass.

'What are you talking about?'

And so she told me.

Dad and his co-workers had met at the appointed spot at the Hamilton Wharves. The organisers had given certain men placards with various slogans and demands printed on them. Dad was given one which read: I CAN'T FEED MY KIDS ON MY WAGES. Large numbers of police had been called in. Many rode horses and the ones on foot carried truncheons in their hands. They formed a barricade of blue in front of the gates leading to the wharves.

One of the men who was near Dad pointed and shouted as a large expensive car pulled up at the gates. Four well-dressed men stepped out.

'There they are! The pannos!' the man shouted.

'Boo! Boo! Rotten panno bastards!' several of the wharfies shouted.

These pannos were the executives who ran the shipping companies in Brisbane. They were called pannos because of their distinctive panama hats.

Dad was right in the thick of it. His voice could be heard clearly. 'They don't know what it's like to break their backs for an honest day's...' And the words died in his throat. Standing tall and proud in the middle of the group of pannos was a man whom Dad recognised. He was wearing a dark suit, odd for the summer heat and a light blue tie and white shirt. And the panama hat, of course. It was a face Dad had wanted to forget but never could. When Dad stopped mid-sentence, the other wharfies around him looked at him, puzzled. Dad averted his face but it was too late. He had singled himself out and the man with the blue tie turned to look. When he saw Dad, a small unpleasant smile crossed his lips.

Dad pulled the placard down in an effort to cover his face. He tried to shrink back from the front line of the group but he could go nowhere because he was hemmed in. Then the panno broke from his group and approached Dad. Several of the police made a move to go with him as the man approached the strikers. But the man waved them away. He seemed to fear nothing. The group around Dad quieted down as the man came forward. This was completely unexpected.

The man stood inches away from Dad. 'I thought it was you. Yes, I knew it was. It must be twenty years but I never forget a face. It was back in the bush. Near Charleville, remember? Sure you do.'

Dad was speechless.

'Let me remind you. Last time I saw you, you were on your knees. You were looking up at me. I even remember how much I paid you. You were worth every penny.'

'I don't know what you're talking about, you rotten panno bastard.'

'Oh, yes, you do. I'll tell you what I'll do. I'll give you what I paid you back then. You never know, you might be able to use the money during this strike. I think it's going to be a long one.'

He took some coins from his pocket and held them out for Dad, who looked at the money but could say nothing. The man let the coins fall from his hand one by one and they landed at Dad's feet.

'Just like the old days, eh?' the man said. He gave a short, nasty laugh, turned and walked back towards his group.

'What is that bastard talking about?' one of the men near Dad said.

Dad could bear it no longer. He pushed the men aside with his elbows and charged forward. 'Bloodsuckers!' he screamed as he ran, waving his placard like the weapon it had suddenly become.

But he got only a few feet from his own group. The police locked arms and moved forward to prevent Dad from getting anywhere. One of them punched him hard in the chest and Dad went to the ground.

The other men saw this and ran to pick Dad up. A donnybrook broke out. Whistles and sirens and the sounds of whinnying horses could be heard. It was a melee of anger and confusion and hatred. Dad was almost trampled underfoot but some of the other men managed to pull him out of the way. About twenty men were arrested for civil disturbance before order was maintained. Luckily, Dad wasn't one of them.

On his way home from the demonstration, Dad did not have the strength to resist the pleadings of his mates to join them at the International Hotel to drown their collective sorrows.

'So,' Mum said, 'his ghosts have come back to haunt him.'

'But, Mum, what did the man mean by "You were on your knees"?'

'Darling, your father had to do something to get some money to eat. He...well, that man was obviously one of those men who liked...he was willing to pay young men...'

I did what I suspect most young people do when a parent attempts to explain such things. 'I think I know what he was doing, Mum. You don't have to tell me any more.'

'I hope so, luvvie,' she said. 'It was painful and he can't quite deal with it. But I've told you this in the hopes that you will never use it against him. This is our secret.'

I nodded my head.

'Okay?' she pressed.

'I promise.'

'I'll do what I can to deflect the blows your father hurls at you but you can, you must, be bigger than your father. I'll always protect you.'

'Thank you, Mum.'

She smiled and bent forward and kissed the top of my head.

We sat and said nothing and ate our carrots. As I tossed the green stalk from the carrot into our small compost heap, I turned to Mum.

'Do you know the first time I remember you protecting me? You probably don't remember.'

'What are you talking about?' she asked.

'Oh, it was when I was very little. The Christmas pageant at St Stephen's.'

'And the miracle jacket?'

I nodded. She remembered.

In my last year at the convent school, I was selected to be in a Christmas pageant. The stage at the end of the large schoolroom was decorated by the nuns to form a stable with the manger in the centre. The most beautiful girl in the school was asked to play Mary and the biggest boy, Joseph. Baby Jesus was a doll. My role was to come in and give a present to the baby Jesus. I wasn't one of the three Wise Men. I don't know who I was supposed to be exactly. I think I was a shepherd. That would make sense given that placed alongside Mary and Joseph were several statues of sheep which had been borrowed from the church's Christmas crèche supplies.

My part called for me to wear an old jacket which the

nuns had dug out from somewhere to make me look a bit more scruffy than usual. Unfortunately, I had taken it home the night before to show Mum and Dad and, when I reached the area where we were all to dress and prepare on the day of the pageant, I realised that I had forgotten to bring my jacket. I was terrified. If the nuns found out that I had left part of my costume at home, I would be in deep trouble. What to do?

I wandered around to the other side of the school. Hanging from a clothes peg on the wall was a jacket that could have been a twin of the one I was to wear! This was nothing short of a miracle. Who else would have put it there but Jesus? I took it, put it on and it was a perfect fit. The show, with me in it, could go on.

I made my entrance from the side of the stage and headed towards the centre where the manger was set up and where Mary and Joseph were kneeling in the hay behind the baby doll, Jesus. I fell to my knees at the sight of the baby doll Jesus and then gave Him my present. I had to make a big deal of my present because that was part of the moral of the story we were portraying. Some people make a big fuss over what they give and that is not a good thing. I was supposed to be such an unworthy person.

I showed Mary and Joseph what I had given. They

nodded and then went back to their praying. I had given them bottle caps. However, through the sheer mastery of my stage performance, I convinced the audience that what I was really offering was priceless diamonds. How a poor shepherd boy with a ratty little miraculous jacket could get his hands on a bunch of diamonds and then give them away to some little baby he hadn't heard of until ten minutes earlier was not at issue. I stood and moved to the side of the stage and took my place with the others who had entered before me and done the same thing, with more or less aplomb.

Next to enter the stage were the three Magi who were dressed in the finest and most colourful robes the nuns could assemble. Their entrances were elaborately grand. They, too, laid their extravagant presents at the feet of the baby Jesus. That would be the gold, frankincense and myrrh. And they too, made much of their presentation of it. They stepped to one side and watched the other kids come on and do the same thing.

The whole idea behind the pageant was that bells and chimes would ring offstage when the baby Jesus was pleased with the present or, more precisely, the manner in which it was given—that is to say, with humility and with great, great love. Last to make an appearance was a sad, tattered little girl who came onstage with a measly little present which she timidly laid at the feet of the baby Jesus. She made no show of what she had given. We were all to indicate that her present was really too pathetic for words. What was she doing here anyway? Step aside. Look at the stuff we gave Him. But she stayed put, bowed her head meekly and prayed.

BONG! BONG! BONG! The chimes rang! Those of us who hadn't caused the chimes to ring were, at that very moment, supposed to look at each other and gasp as loudly as we could. We were to look horrified and puzzled. How could our beautiful presents not make the chimes ring? We were to look at the person next to us and mouth something like, 'There must be some mistake here.' Or, 'Do you think the gong person has suddenly gone mad?'

I took one look at the kid next to me and saw that his beard had slipped. He, poor wretch, was blissfully unaware of it. I took my deep breath and gasped. But I overdid it. My intake of breath was so big that wisps of his twisted beard got caught in my mouth. I started to choke and tried to spit it out but it kept catching and sticking to my teeth. Then the piece that hooked over his right ear came free. His beard was now dangling from one ear, sort of at half-mast.

I started to giggle. And then my bearded friend started

to giggle and then one or two others started to giggle. Before we knew it, Mary, Joseph, the three Magi and the supporting lesser players were in hysterics. Parents started to laugh. Baby brothers and sisters in the audience laughed as well.

The much-feared Sister Mary Alphonsus did not laugh. The chimes went merrily on. BONG! BONG! BONG! The more they rang, the funnier that, too, became. The pageant was by now in tatters.

The curtain came down. Sister Mary Alphonsus arrived in a cloud of dust and fury and stood with hands on hips before her terrified cast.

'You have ruined the Christmas pageant!' she roared. 'The baby Jesus is terribly offended. Tony Fingleton, step over to me!'

The sight of Sister Mary Alphonsus, veins fairly popping on her face, rendered me motionless. I stood glued to the spot.

'Come here at once!' It was a bark that might make grown men wince.

But before I took a step a second miracle occurred on that day. Mum came over to me and took my hand which I grasped as hard as I had ever grasped anything in my life.

'It was a beautiful pageant, sister,' Mum said. 'You

must be so pleased with the way it turned out. Everyone was so happy when the little orphan girl was able to make the bells ring. What a wonderful idea to have everybody be so happy when it happened!'

Sister Mary Alphonsus looked at my mother, then at me and then at us all.

'You're all to go over to the church immediately and say ten Hail Marys and ten Our Fathers!' she barked.

Chastened, we headed for the church. As we walked, Mum bent down to me. 'I thought you were absolutely wonderful,' she whispered in my ear. 'You stole the show.'

I think I loved her as much at that moment as I ever did in my life. I have to think that the baby Jesus might have found it a little amusing, too.

'I still think you stole the show that day,' Mum said now.

I nodded. Perhaps she was right.

'I've got ironing to do and I suppose I have to see if your father's up. He'll probably have an awful hangover. God knows what's in store today. Oh, dear.'

'Thanks, Mum.'

She blew me a kiss and made her way to the back stairs.

chapter 11

'He would never have said anything like that to Harold,' I told John. 'Or to you.'

'You have to forget it,' he echoed Mum.

We stood in the shallow end pushing the kickboard back and forth between us.

'Would you be able to forget it?'

He shook his head 'no' and tears filled his eyes. 'I'd never do anything to hurt you, Tony. Ever.'

'I know you wouldn't.'

We did our handshake again, this time much slower because we both felt such pain. But John broke it suddenly to scoop up a handful of water and fling it at me. We splashed water at each other for a furious few seconds and then dived under and swam to the other end of the pool.

The drinking became part of our lives. After Dad got up that first morning and had something to eat and several cups of tea, he went off. Mum begged him to stay home but he left. There seemed to be an urgency about getting back to the pub. It was almost as if he had many years to catch up on, as if he were suddenly liberated. His promise to Mum was no longer valid. He had signed his own release form.

The strike finished a few days later, but Dad kept drinking.

Once Dad started drinking, it dominated and controlled his life. The binges became daily affairs and, worse, nightly affairs. Sometimes, he would simply stop without warning. And then start up again. I often wondered which was worse—the drinking or the lull, as it were, before the storm. What quickly became obvious to us all was that, like most alcoholics, if Dad wasn't drinking, he was thinking about it.

How he managed to drag himself to work some mornings was nothing short of superhuman. When he would give it up for a spell, it seemed to come from the sheer exhaustion of his keeping up with it. He would look so worn out. Mum would serve him cup after cup of tea. He would lie in bed for long periods and sleep. Mum was constantly at his side to make sure that, if he needed anything, she would get it for him. Her goal was to keep him happy so that he would not start pacing and leave the house. But while he was trying to get off the booze, we were under strict instruction from Mum not to do anything that might upset him and send him back to the pub. We obeyed because we wanted the dry spell almost as much as he wanted it for himself.

But he always went back to it. If he was at work, the air at home would be electric with tension. We would wait for him, eyes on the clock. A minute past his usual time to come home. Two minutes now. Five. Maybe he was delayed, we told ourselves. The trams are slow. Nobody believed it even as they said it. And then we would know what lay in store. He was on it again. And we would wait; we would wait until he came home stumbling drunk, knocking into things, swearing and lashing out at Mum. We hated him for it.

He was not a happy drunk. He was a maudlin, noisy, violent drunk who terrified us. He would bring home a supply of bottles and not go to bed until he had drunk them all. He'd be up all night. Mum sat up with him, commiserating, cajoling, begging him to go to bed, not to keep us awake. But he wouldn't. She sat up and listened as Dad talked and talked, rehashing the horror stories from his youth. Or he sang songs all night long, mostly the same ones, over and over. I grew to loathe 'When Irish Eyes Are Smiling' and 'Too-ra-loo-ra-loo-rah'. Bing Crosby has a lot to answer for in my book. I grew to hate him too.

We never sat up with Dad and listened to his stories. All they did was keep us awake. We had school the next day or we had to be up at 5.30 to go to the pool. While he was drinking, he was incapable of overseeing our training sessions so we were on our own and we resented it.

Dad began to turn up at our swimming events after spending a good part of the day at the pub. He would lurch in, making a noisy entrance. He talked loudly to people as he teetered his way to where we were sitting. He would climb to the top row of seats at the Valley Pool and weave dangerously along it. If one of us was waiting to swim in a race, or doing backstroke and hence could see while swimming, our eyes wouldn't leave him. Would he fall, hurt himself, start a fight or shout abuse? At Mum? He never came in quietly or tried to cover his obvious state of inebriation and our pain was palpable. There was even one disastrous evening when he fell in the pool, much to the amusement of everybody else except us.

Money was now an even bigger problem than before. Mum bore the brunt of it. How could she pay the bills? The little that might have been left over once upon a time was now handed to the publican at the International Hotel.

Mum scrimped and tried to stretch the grocery money as far as she could but after a particularly difficult time with the local grocer, she'd had enough. She was determined to shame Dad into giving up the drinking so that she wouldn't have to beg for more credit.

She decided to visit the public bar at the International Hotel.

The pubs closed early in those days, giving rise to the ritual of the six o'clock swill, when men drank as much as they could with their mates before closing time. We watched from the footpath through the open windows. A deadly hush fell over the bar as soon as Mum stepped into this male *sanctum sanctorum*. To all appearances blissfully unaware of the silence, she looked around for Dad.

A burly labourer immediately stepped into her path. 'Lose something, missus?'

'Yes, my husband.' Mum tried to move around him,

still looking for Dad. But the burly man stepped with her, blocking her from going further. 'Step out of my way,' Mum said.

'Men's only bar, missus.'

'If I have to go and get the police to come in here, I will. Judging by the look of you, I would suspect that they might want to have a word or two with the likes of you,' she said. The man stepped back. Mum spotted Dad sitting at the bar, alone. She walked over to him.

'I want you to come home, now, Harold.'

You could hear a pin drop. It must have been a day when Dad was not working because, from his state of inebriation, he had been drinking for many hours. He was far gone. His head was lolling forward. One hand was holding the bottom of his half-drunk glass of beer. The glass rested on a copy of the *Telegraph*, Brisbane's evening newspaper. Mum looked at it. There was a picture of John on the back page, taken after a race where he had set yet another state record. There was a wet ring on the picture.

'Your kid's picture is in the paper and that's all it means to you? A place to put your filthy glass of beer?'

Dad barely lifted his head. 'Turn it up, Dora. Go home.'

'Not until you come with me.'

'Leave your old man alone, missus. He deserves his fun,' a patron called across at Mum.

'He does? Why? When am I entitled to have my fun?' She pointed to one of the men, a labourer in dirty shorts and a very dirty dark blue singlet. 'Why aren't you at home with your wife and children?'

This was greeted with loud guffaws.

'I bet your wife would love to have what you've spent in here today. Imagine. She might even be able to buy herself a decent pair of shoes.'

'She'll get a new pair of shoes when I'm bloody good and ready to give her the money to buy a new pair of shoes.'

More guffaws. Tommy Thurman, who was sitting on the far side of the bar, walked to Mum and took her to one side. Mum resisted and pulled her arm from his grasp.

'I can't afford to buy food for the kids, Tommy,' she said. 'He spends all his money in this filthy place.'

'I know, Dora. I know. I'll try to get him to go home after he finishes the beer he's got in front of him.'

'Where is it going to end? It's worse than it was when you two were single and running around town.'

'He's trying to drown something he can't drown.'

Mum nodded. 'He's got to stop. Help me, will you, Tommy?'

Tommy nodded and stood beside Dad and rested his hand on Dad's back. Dad looked up blearily and nodded to his old friend.

'Maybe you should make this one the last one, Harold. What do you reckon?'

Mum leaned into Dad again. 'Come home, Harold.'

'You're making a fool of me. Leave me alone.'

Mum looked around her at the men who continued to look at her as if she were some alien being. She sensed that she was not only losing the battle but the war as well.

'You should be ashamed of yourselves, the lot of you,' she said.

'Another round here, Mavis.' Loud laughter.

Mum shook her head. She was disgusted. By this time I was inside the bar and tugging at her hand. She nodded and we walked out together.

The routine was now firmly established. Dad would drink until he stopped. No pleading from any of us helped. Mum grew more and more desperate as the toll on her began to show.

Soon after this, Billie asked Mum to join her in a smart restaurant right in town in the main shopping area. I came along to keep her company. It was called

The Shingle Inn and was an olde-English style tea and sandwiches place with a decidedly 'uptown' air. We thought it looked like a marvellous place but we never went in because we couldn't afford it. We made do with the aromas that emanated from its dignified interior and they were intoxicating. The confections in the windows were masterpieces of gastronomic whimsy. There were large cakes and cupcakes, creamily enticing with fanciful toppings, as well as white floury scones and pastries of varying shapes and sizes.

When she was seated with Billie at one of the tables, Mum ogled the cake trolley as a waitress wheeled it around the room. This was another touch that made The Shingle Inn special. The waitresses wore smart black uniforms with highly starched white aprons and stiff white caps like a cross between a nurse's cap and a tiara. They were engineering marvels.

Billie came right to the point. 'Leave him, Dora. I could talk to my solicitor. He could help you.'

Mum gave Billie one of her dubious looks.

'The kids need a father. He's better than nothing.'

'Is he?'

'Sometimes...' My mother began to drift into another time when things were happier. 'Do you know I've known him all my life? I can't remember a time when I didn't. We were kids together. He always struck me as the saddest person I'd ever known but I suppose what attracted me to him was that little bit of danger in him. You know? And he was so handsome. You have no idea how handsome he was when he was young.'

'He still is.'

'Where would we go if I left him, Billie? Where would he go? Like it or not, I'm Harold's wife. I'm his children's mother. And Billie, that's all I ever wanted to be.'

Billie took some money out of her purse. It was money for some ironing that Mum was now taking in from Billie. Mum was also doing laundry and ironing for a woman in Torrington Street not far from the Spring Hill Baths. With so much of Dad's pay going to the pubs, Mum had to find a way to supplement what little he gave her.

He always hid his money at night. He never seemed too drunk to do that. He hid it because Mum had resorted to going through his pockets at night for loose change when he was asleep.

'I almost forgot to give you this. I wish it were more.' She handed Mum ten pounds which was as much as Dad might earn sometimes in a week. Mum squirrelled it away in her purse.

'Oh, but this is lovely. I've already got it earmarked

for Christmas next week.'

'If you did leave him, he'd have to support you, you know.'

'I think that comes under the heading that if you live long enough, you'll hear just about everything.'

Billie signalled the waitress with the trolley of cakes. 'Let's have one of each. To hell with my waistline.'

Mum reached across and touched Billie's arm. 'I wish you understood,' she said.

'I do but I don't want to.'

'I know,' Mum said sadly. 'No one does.'

Christmas that year was a tough one. Out of the blue and with no explanation, Dad stopped drinking. He brooded and he was edgy. He hated Christmas.

Mum loved it. A week or so before Christmas Day, the house was decorated with bunting and streamers. We had green and red streamers made of some kind of synthetic material that formed the basis of our decorating. Little black and silver pine cones were interspersed at various intervals along them. Mum put these away each year and brought them out again the next, and they were greeted like old friends. We draped these around the living room walls. Mum also bought several packages of coloured crepe paper at

Woolworth's. It was then our job—and it was a fun one—to cut this paper into two-inch strips and create streamers with them. This was done by folding one piece over another and then unfolding it so it became a twirled piece of paper craftsmanship. We pinned the strips together for the required length and hung them from corner to corner.

Dad highly disapproved of 'all this bloody messy crap around the house'.

On Christmas morning, Santa Claus left our presents in a pillow case beside our beds. Miraculously, Mum had scrimped and saved enough to buy us games and books or toys. Each of us received a new article of clothing. She began saving for Christmas on the day after Christmas. She must have had her own safety deposit box hidden somewhere but we never knew where. That money was untouchable. With it, she also bought special food which always included a chicken for our lunch. Chicken was a luxury. We had it twice a year—at Christmas and Easter. There were nuts and plenty of summer fruits like plums, apricots, peaches and cherries. Mum set them all out on the sideboard. We could eat as much as we wanted whenever we wanted. Set up on the back verandah was a washing tub filled with ice where there were numerous bottles of our favourite soft drinks.

Christmas dinner was held in the middle of the day. Once the presents were opened, Mum started preparing the meal. In the sweltering heat, she roasted the chicken and pounds of potatoes and vegetables and gravy. When everything was prepared, we were called in and took our places at the dining table in the living room. The table was resplendent with a flower arrangement and party favours. Mum had carved the chicken herself and set the potatoes and vegetables on our plates. Everything looked wonderful. But there was one person missing from the table.

'Harold,' Mum called. 'Christmas dinner is ready. Would you come in now?'

We sat expectant and fearful. There was no sound coming from Mum and Dad's bedroom where Dad had spent most of the morning.

'God, what a feast!' I said.

John said, 'This is a great Christmas, Mum.'

'I got everything I wanted,' Ronald said.

'I can't wait to eat,' John said.

We dared not start. Mum turned to my brother, Harold.

'Go and get your father.'

Harold got up and went into Dad's bedroom. He reappeared a moment later.

'Did you tell him?'

Harold nodded and took his place. 'He didn't say anything.'

A moment or two later Dad walked into the living room. His face was cold.

Diane spoke up. 'It's chicken, Dad. It's the most beautiful meal I've ever seen.'

Dad looked at her and then across at Mum. His eyes were dead. 'Is this what my breaking back pays for?'

'I've been saving.'

'I never had a Christmas when I was a kid. Here's what I think of it now.'

Never taking his eyes off Mum, Dad picked up his plate by the rim and flipped it completely over in its place. We all winced as if we had been slapped.

'I don't want anything to eat. Leave me the hell alone.'

He turned and went back towards his room. There wasn't a sound until one of the balloons in the cluster that we had hung in a corner burst. It was like a cannon going off. We all jumped and Diane let out a squeal of fright. Dad didn't stop and went into his room. Then his door slammed and we jumped once more.

There were tears pouring down Mum's face. We all rushed to her side.

'I'll be fine. Sit down. Sit down. Let's eat our dinner

before it gets cold. Though in this heat, that won't happen for a while.'

We forced a little laugh and went back to our places and started the meal. Mum turned Dad's plate right side up, scraped the food back on it and took it to the kitchen. When she returned, she had a cloth napkin which she flapped open and placed over the spot in Dad's place to hide the stain. About halfway through the meal, I nodded to Diane. She reached under the table and took what I had in my hand. I had seen it at Woolworth's and we all thought Mum would like it. She liked smelly things and we all agreed that this package of three soaps, a hand lotion, a shampoo and a can of powder would make her happy. Diane presented it to her.

'This is a little something from all of us, Mum. Tony told us that none of us is allowed to use the soap. It's all for you.'

Mum took it and the smile on her face made everything in the world seem all right. 'Oh, it's too lovely,' she said. She put the package to her nose and took in its aromas. 'Ooh, I'm going to smell so good.'

She looked around at the five beaming faces.

'Thank you all. What a perfect present.' She raised her glass of soft drink. 'Merry Christmas, my darlings.'

'Merry Christmas, Mum.'

part 3

DAWN FRASER TRIPS THE LIGHT FANTASTIC WITH TONY 1962

chapter 12

1956 was a big year in Australia. Melbourne was to host
the Olympic Games in November. It was the first time
that a nation in the southern hemisphere would host the
Olympics and the entire country was in a state of
excitement.

In late January, the Australian Swimming
Championships were to be held in Sydney. The results
would determine the Australian team that would go to
the Olympics.

By this time, I was the best backstroke swimmer my
age in Queensland. I had won the State Junior (Under-
Sixteen) Championship and was a member of the

Queensland team that would compete in the Australian Championships. It would only be the second time I had ever been outside Queensland.

'We'll all go to Sydney,' Dad told us. 'We'll stay with Molly in Paddington and see Tony's race.'

Molly was Dad's only sister. As brutal as Dad could be at times, Aunty Molly was the opposite. Gentle, kind, religious and generous. She lived with another woman most of her adult life, a woman we called Aunty Lucy who was a registered nurse. We only pieced the meaning of this together in later years and Mum, who was generally liberal about such matters, verified it for us. Visits to Aunty Molly's house were treasured times in our family because things there were ordered and cultured. We adored her.

As a member of the Queensland team I would fly to Sydney. The rest of the family, with the exception of my brother, Harold, would take the train. It was an historic first for our family to take such a trip. Mercifully, Dad was still off the booze.

Dad had read in one of the newspapers that a young boy in Sydney was being heralded as the best swimmer his age in Australia. Like John, he was twelve and his times were roughly the same. This infuriated Dad. He arranged with the boy's father in Sydney that John and his son should race in the North Sydney Pool one morning during the week-long Australian Championships. Dad arranged for a starter to be there to 'officiate'. He arranged with the caretakers of the pool itself to allow this 'event' to take place. How he did all this, without the benefit of a telephone—which we did not own—was a mystery to us but it was impressive.

John won the race. It was no contest. His time was faster over fifty metres than any other boy his age had recorded in Australia. It made Dad's trip to Sydney. He thought he had the next big star in the world of swimming.

The Australian Championships that year were thrilling. Australian swimmers were the best in the world and the attention and adulation they received were extraordinary. Many of them lopped seconds off world records almost every time they competed. They were golden, glorious gods to me.

Murray Rose, Jon Henricks and John Devitt were enormously famous figures of that time. Dawn Fraser and Lorraine Crapp were like movie stars. They would go on and win a record number of medals, gold, silver and bronze, in the Melbourne Olympics.

I won my race and became Australian Junior Backstroke Champion and it was a very big deal. For me. And for Mum and the others. But not necessarily for

Dad. His reaction paled in comparison to the thrill he'd got from John's beating the young boy from Sydney in the arranged race. That was the way of it.

By now my brother Harold shared very little of our lives. He never came to see us swim. He never asked how we fared. He never mentioned having seen an article in the newspaper about us. He was trying to find his own way by playing football for the local team in winter and, in summer, he joined a surf life-saving club at Tallebudgera Beach on Queensland's South Coast. Every Friday after work as an apprentice bricklayer, he was driven to the clubhouse at Tallebudgera and received training in life-guard duties on Saturday and Sunday.

This seemed a good idea at the time, because it gave Harold a certain direction and a place to go to each weekend. Mum and Dad thought he would gain some sense of independence and responsibility by living with young men and sharing the duties of guarding the surfing beaches.

On Saturday nights, many of these young men frequented the pubs. Harold needed very little encouragement from the other members to join them on these forays.

Not long after we returned from Sydney, we were, as was usual on a Sunday night, sitting around the radio with Tommy Thurman listening to one of our favourite programs. There was a loud thud, followed by the ringing of our front door bell. We all sat bolt upright. We weren't expecting anyone. We hurried to the front door. It was almost identical to Dad's dramatic entrance when he came home drunk those many harrowing moons ago, except this time, there was my brother, Harold.

Harold was being held between two young men. Neither of them could have been older than eighteen or nineteen. Harold's arms were flung around their shoulders. He was dead drunk. The boys tried to put Harold down but his weight was too much for them and he slipped to the floor. The four of us peered out from behind Mum who did not immediately move to him because she was in such a state of shock. When she did, she held Harold's head and looked up at the two boys.

'I suppose you're proud of yourselves. You've gotten this boy rotten drunk. He's only sixteen!'

'It wasn't our fault, Mrs Fingleton. There was nothing we could do to stop him. It was what he wanted.'

Mum apologised.

'We can't control him,' she said. 'I don't see how I can expect you to.'

'How did he get served in the pub?' Dad asked.

'You know how that works, Mr Fingleton. We just passed the beers out through the window.'

'I've done it myself,' Dad said. 'Thanks for bringing him home.' He turned to the rest of us. 'Go to bed.'

'Does he have to do everything you do?' Mum said.

chapter 13

I wanted one day to become Australian Backstroke Champion, and to compete in the Olympics. I was too young to compete in Melbourne but perhaps I could make it to Rome in 1960. I was prepared to make the sacrifices to achieve the goals I set for myself.

Up and back in the pool I went, counting off the laps. If I was doing eight four hundreds, for example, I would count one number for the number of four hundreds I was doing and then another number for the lap count. So it went like this: 'One, one. One, two. One, three.' Until I got to one, sixteen and then I would take a short rest and start in on 'Two, one. Two, two. Two, three.' If, heaven forbid, I lost count, it would be: 'Was that three, eight or three, ten?' After a while, I'd just say 'To hell with it. It's three, eight and if I do two laps more, so what?'

And that's how I spent a large part of my day. Mornings from six until about eight and afternoons from five until seven. Sometimes as many as eleven or twelve kilometres a day.

I knew I was good. I also knew I wasn't great. If I wanted to go all the way in swimming, and I did, I would have to work harder than the next guy. Swimming and the recognition I got from it became who I was. It defined me as much as anything else did.

'I have to keep swimming. I don't have anything else,' I told Mum.

'That's because you don't have the confidence to know that just being you is enough. Believe me, it is. I couldn't care less if you want to be an Australian Champion. I love you for what you are.'

I plugged along, quietly, always in the shadow of my brother. John got better and better and faster and faster. He broke records. But then he began to shirk on his training. If Dad wasn't around, he didn't work as hard as I did. It was at the Queensland Championships when John was fifteen that everything about our swimming careers took an unexpected turn and, as far as our relationship was concerned, an even more disastrous one.

John and I had always been close. Intimate in the best way. We shared so many things besides our swimming and we loved each other. Together we bore the brunt of Dad's tempers and demands as far as swimming was concerned. We knew the depth of each other's pain when Dad arrived at the pool in a drunken, dishevelled and abusive state. It had become a standard practice to give each other our handshake before the other's event. We barely thought about it, so automatic was it by this time.

In 1958, John was, as usual, heavily favoured to win the Junior (Under-Sixteen) State Freestyle Championship. He finished fifth. It was an incomprehensible defeat for Dad. He was devastated.

Dad stormed out of the pool. As we followed, we saw him enter the pub a short distance away. John decided that he would attempt to explain himself.

'You rotten little cur,' Dad hissed at John as he saw him enter the bar.

'Sorry, Dad,' John said. 'They were just too good.'

'Too good? No, they weren't too good. They trained. You didn't. You don't have the guts to work hard enough. You think all you have to do is show up and you'll win? Find someone else to train you. I've had enough of this swimming business.'

In the months that followed John's first major defeat, Dad drank and then he didn't drink. Harold, my brother, drank and drank. The only breaks from Harold's drinking occurred during the week because he had to work.

One night, when Harold was about nineteen, he walked into the kitchen miserably drunk. Dad was already ensconced there at his usual spot at the kitchen table, a glass of beer and an open bottle in front of him. He had been drinking for much of the day and night.

Dad looked up as Harold lurched in. 'Look at this little no-hoper!'

Harold spat back, 'What about you? Who are you calling a no-hoper? You're the biggest no-hoper of them all. What have you ever done that was so great?'

'Bringing you into the world certainly wasn't so great, you useless little bludger!'

'All we've ever heard all our lives is how great a football player you were. What have you got to prove it? You're nothing!'

Mum stepped between them. 'I want you to go to bed, Harold,' she said to my brother.

'Who does he think he is to sit around and judge people?'

'I'll show you who…'

Dad let fly with a punch to Harold's head. Harold fell to the floor but was up in an instant and threw himself at Dad. Mum sandwiched herself somewhere between them. Fists flew out, over and around her. Then, in a flash, all three of them landed in a heap on the floor. They probably slipped on spilled beer. Several bottles fell and crashed to the floor. Shards of glass flew everywhere.

The four of us had, by this time, bolted from our beds and run to the kitchen to see what the tumult was. Diane began to cry. John and Ronald stood by powerless to do anything.

Mum called over her shoulder. 'Tony, throw all the knives out the window!'

A chill ran through me. 'Knives!' I thought. 'Yes, they're angry enough to kill each other.'

I jumped over the three writhing bodies and yanked the entire drawer out of the cabinet and tossed it through the open window. At that point, Mum tried to pull Harold's head back. He was still flailing out with punches at Dad. The three younger ones stood at the kitchen door watching the battle on the floor at their feet in horror. I saw them, as one, make a move to come into the kitchen.

'No!' I yelled.

Mum's eyes also caught their movement. 'Stay there!' she screamed. Somehow, in the struggle, her forefinger slipped into Harold's mouth as she tried to pull back on his head. Harold thought it was Dad's finger and bit down on it. Blood shot everywhere.

'Harold!' Mum screamed. 'That's my finger! I think you've bitten it off! Stop! Stop!'

But Mum held on tight to whatever she was holding onto, most likely one of Dad's arms. She must have thought letting go would be even worse. Dad and Harold were oblivious to Mum's pain and the blood that was spurting everywhere. The three of them were covered in it. It seemed like there was blood all over the kitchen. I thought that somebody was going to die.

Finally, Mum's screams that she had lost a finger and the noise from the rest of us made Dad and Harold stop long enough for me to jump into the fray and, with all the strength in my body, pull Harold away from Mum and Dad. I hauled him to the back door. He was still flailing and grunting and heaving and kicking like some wild animal. How I managed it I'll never know because he was stronger than I was and completely enraged. I got him out the door and closed and locked it quickly after him.

We all ran to Mum and helped her to her feet. She held her hand up above her heart and collapsed into a chair. Blood oozed down her arm but the finger was still there. Dad just stood and looked at the blood.

'Quickly, get a towel to stanch the flow of blood,' I yelled at John. John darted to the sink and ran the dish-cloth under the water. He brought it to me and I showed him how to hold it carefully around the wound.

'I'm going to the telephone across the street to call the ambulance.'

I called the General Hospital and told them what had happened. I was frantic. I ran back to the house. Diane was, by this time, hysterical—such a little girl to be seeing so much horror in her own home. For days after, she was sick to her stomach.

Thankfully, the ambulance arrived within minutes. I went with Mum to the hospital where she received numerous stitches. She was in pain for many weeks later. She never had the complete use of the finger for the rest of her life.

Later, John said that during the course of the fight he suggested to Ronald and Diane that they pray to God for the fight to end. None of us gave any credit to God for interceding, but it did stop. Harold went down the back stairs and made his way through the front door to his room and promptly fell asleep. Dad too collapsed in his bed, leaving John, Ronald and Diane to clean up the mess. After that, Dad stopped drinking for a while.

By now, at the end of the fifties, I was nineteen and John seventeen. I had graduated from Gregory Terrace and was a student teacher. It was a sensible choice because there was no way that Dad could or would send any of us on to university after our senior year at high school. I enjoyed teaching and it provided the family with extra income. I paid Mum for room and board and planned to live at home until I might marry.

I still trained hard and enjoyed being chosen each year to participate in the Australian Championships. But John was no longer the unparalleled star he had once been. Other young men challenged him and it became increasingly difficult for him. Then, during one of our training sessions, he swam backstroke alongside me. He was good at it, and Dad noticed it. He began to train John in secret.

I don't remember there being any announcement at home about it, but John's name was there in the program listed alongside mine when the Queensland Championships came around in 1959. I was a wreck. Competing against my little brother was not a possibility I had ever imagined. I was nervous before even the most minor club meet when I knew all I had to do was to stay afloat and I would win. When I lined up behind the blocks, I couldn't look at John. My mouth was dry and I could barely speak. If I'd had anything in my stomach, I would have thrown it up.

John beat me and I fell apart. And I felt betrayed.

I had nowhere to turn and I thought I had hit the end of my swimming road. It wasn't just that John had beaten me. Instinctively, I knew he was a better swimmer than I was. And all he had to do was to keep working and he would take the path that I had hoped would be mine. He now had the edge physically and psychologically.

I remember the ride home in the car after that race. Dad was elated. John was happy because Dad was happy and he was State Champion. At my grand age of nineteen, I felt old and ridiculous. John Konrads and his sister Ilsa had become overnight sensations in swimming at the ages of sixteen and fourteen, breaking world records by seconds. Swimming was a sport for kids.

The following day, I couldn't speak to anyone and I didn't want to.

'So, how long are you going to feel sorry for yourself?' Mum said to me.

'Mum, come on,' I said. 'Dad wants John to win. And he did. John's the star of the family. But swimming's all I can do. I've worked so hard. I hoped I could become somebody.'

'Darling, if you're not somebody without a medal, you're still nobody with one.'

'Mum, I had this dream—maybe it was a stupid dream but it was my dream, you know? I thought that maybe if I got to the top in swimming, it could lead to something. I could get away, go somewhere.'

Mum tapped the side of her head. 'Up here,' she said. 'That's where you have to win. You're depressed and you're angry. At your father and at John. Well, good. Build on it! Use it!'

I had no idea what she was driving at.

'Your anger will give you the strength to go on from here.'

'I don't know…'

'I love you and I'm proud of you. Why do you think the younger ones always turn to you? Why do you think I lean on you so much when your father is so difficult to live with?'

'What's that got to do with anything? This is different. I wanted to be the best backstroke swimmer in Australia.'

'So do it! You're the only one who can make something of yourself. Not your father. Not me. You! If swimming's what you want, well, there's next year. Don't ever look back. Look to the future and rely on yourself.'

She turned and walked away without saying another word.

chapter 14

I decided I would train again the following year and see what would come of it. The Rome Olympics in 1960 loomed and I would aim for a spot on the Australian team. It would be an uphill battle because of the tough competition but I thought I had a chance.

The days melded into each other and I slogged away at the boring routine of morning and afternoon sessions. One afternoon around five thirty, as I was passing the International Hotel on my way home, I heard a familiar voice from out of the window.

'Hey! Come in here and have a beer with me.' It was my brother, Harold.

I didn't like beer much but drank it occasionally with my friends. In fact, the first time I drank beer, I threw up. After only the first glass. And I was afraid that if I did acquire a taste for beer, that particular family gene, which seemed to be a dominant one, might take hold in me too.

'Nah,' I said. 'I don't want to drink when I'm training.'

I saw the disappointed look on Harold's face.

'Okay, sure.'

I walked around to the front of the hotel and joined Harold. I rested my towel and swimsuit on the bar and asked the barmaid for a beer. There was a look of bemusement and delight on Harold's face.

'What's this?' Harold said. 'Saint Anthony drinks?'

'Stuff it, Harold,' I said. 'I'd like to have a beer with you without shit getting in the way.'

I took a sip from my glass. We looked at each other as if we were perfect strangers. We had little in common. In all our lives, we had never really communicated with each other in any meaningful way. But there was a bond of some kind or other between us. Common experiences, common knowledge of common events.

'Training hard?' he asked.

'Yeah.'

'Better you than me, mate.'

'I'm over you, you know,' I blurted out. 'But it took me a long time. The bullying, the punches, the name-calling. Why couldn't we have been friends?'

He didn't seem shocked. He gave a short laugh. 'I don't know, Tony,' he said. 'I didn't mean to hurt you. Was it so bad?'

'Harold, it was bloody awful,' I said. 'You became Dad's partner in my misery.'

'Do you have any idea how hard it was to watch you get better and better at swimming?' he asked.

'I worked for it,' I said.

'Yes. But I had nothing.'

'Stop feeling sorry for yourself.'

'I wanted Dad to notice me.'

'So did I.'

We looked at each other.

'You used to piss me off when we were kids,' Harold said finally. 'You were always such a little goodie-goody. I wanted to be the bad boy and you didn't.'

We sat there, looking into our beers.

'Why do you think I'm such a saint?' I said. 'I'm not a saint. I just didn't want to fight with everybody the way you did.'

'I'm sorry, mate. When you started to swim, you and

John, I felt completely left out. So I thought if I out-drank the old man, he'd be impressed.'

He looked hard at me and made a fist and lightly tapped my chin with it. 'Even though I could beat the crap out of you when we were kids, I always knew you were a fighter. You never give up, do you?'

I laughed. This was an enormous compliment. 'Maybe one of these days I'll stop banging my head against the wall. It'll feel pretty good, I reckon.'

'Being a fighter isn't just about slugging it out in a boxing ring, you know.' He put his arm around my neck and squeezed hard. 'Do it on your own, Tony. Do it without the old man. You don't need him. Show him!'

'I will show him, Harold.'

I got up from the stool at the bar and picked up my towel and bathing suit.

'Don't you ever get sick of it? All that training? Back and forth, up and down a bloody pool? Jesus, I couldn't stand it!'

'God, you have no idea how much at times. But I've got to prove something. I only wish I knew what it was.'

I turned to leave.

'Tony...' He grabbed me and hugged me hard. 'Go get 'em, mate.'

chapter 15

Soon after this, Harold took a job in another town.

Dad was drinking again. One night he came home
late and was sitting at the kitchen table with half a dozen
bottles of beer. We'd gone to bed early because we had a
State Championship coming up. We had jammed clothes
at the bottom of the door to keep out the sound of our
father's voice and the dreaded strains of 'When Irish Eyes
Are Smiling'. Mum called through the door that she was
going to bed. We were glad that, for once, she wasn't
going to sit up with Dad to keep him company. What we
didn't know was that later he went into their bedroom
and sat on the side of the bed beside her to get started in

on his familiar litany of torment.

At about two-thirty in the morning, my father pushed his way into our room. The barricade of clothes at the bottom of the door made it difficult for him. I heard his noisy entry and woke up. He stood over me, reeling. He was sloppily drunk.

'Get up,' he said. 'You'd better go and help your mother.'

I sat up. John and Ronald rolled over, not aware that anything was going on.

'Silly bloody woman's swallowed a bottle of sleeping pills,' he said. 'She's tried to commit suicide.'

The hair on the back of my neck stood on end. Suicide! What was he talking about? There is that odd moment right after being awakened from a deep sleep when you think you're dreaming. It took me a moment to comprehend. I wasn't dreaming.

'Mum!' I yelled at the top of my voice and bolted from my bed.

John and Ronald were now wide awake and they, too, leapt from their beds and followed me into Mum's bedroom where we found her lying flat on her back, crying and groggy. Diane burst in behind us. She was petrified. We crowded around our mother's bed.

'What have you done?' we all cried.

'I can't stand it any more, darlings,' she said. 'He's driving me crazy! I just want to die. Let me die.'

Her speech was slurred.

'We've got to get her up!' I yelled at my shaken brothers and sister. 'Help me get her up!'

I looked at Mum. Her head started to roll back and her eyes closed.

'You can't go to sleep! You'll never wake up!'

I grabbed one of her lifeless arms and slung it over my shoulder. John followed suit and did the same with the other one.

'Do you know what you're doing?' John asked.

'I saw something like this at the pictures. We have to keep her awake, no matter how long it takes. The pills have to wear off.'

'Let me lie down,' Mum drawled.

'No!' I barked at her. I was frightened and angry. 'How could you do this?' I asked her.

Diane was now in uncontrollable tears. 'Mum, I don't want you to die!'

'He won't let me sleep. I have to get some sleep.'

And she slumped again. The dead weight of her was making it almost impossible to keep her upright. We walked and dragged her back and forth in her bedroom and then we headed out into the living room. We turned on all the lights. Back and forth. Up and down the hallway. Round and round the dining room table. She kept closing her eyes and her head rolled around on her shoulders and forward on her chest as if she had no control over it, which she didn't. We did this for a few minutes, no more than fifteen, although it seemed like an eternity. I began to realise that we couldn't keep this up.

I turned to Ronald. 'Here, you take her.'

I placed Mum's arm over his shoulder and he and John tried walking her back and forth in the living room. Diane was walking backwards in front of Mum, wiping her forehead with a cold washcloth, all the while tears rolling down her cheeks.

Where was Dad, I wondered? I ran to the front door. There he was sitting on the front steps, his head between his legs. Useless.

'I'm going to the corner to call an ambulance,' I said. 'Tony, don't leave us!' Diane begged.

'Come with me if you like.'

'I don't want to leave Mum,' she said.

Poor little thing. It was more than her twelve-year-old experience could grasp. I held her hard by the shoulders.

'Listen to me,' I said to her. 'You've got to be strong for Mum, okay? Make me proud of you.' She nodded as she sobbed. 'Help John and Ronald. Don't let her rest no matter what. Slap her, pinch her, throw a bucket of water over her, I don't care. Just don't let her sleep.'

I headed for the door.

'Tony!' Diane ran after me and stopped me before I disappeared into the night. 'I could sing to her. She loves to sing. Maybe she'll join in and that will keep her awake.'

'Good. Anything but "Irish Eyes", okay?'

She nodded and tried to smile. I bent down and looked at her. I looked at that pretty little face. Her eyes were too old and too sad for her years. It was not fair. I kissed her on the top of the head and dashed to the public phone on the corner.

Within fifteen minutes, the ambulance arrived and Mum's stomach was pumped out and she was saved. The medics had telephoned the police which they were legally bound to do. The police made their report and left.

We were afraid to leave her in her bedroom but with the assurances of the medics we felt reasonably secure. I sent John and Ronald back to bed but Diane insisted that she stay with Mum and so she curled up on Mum's bed with her. I slept on the rug on the floor, just in case. I don't remember where Dad spent the night.

Mum awoke with a very sore throat and probably something akin to a hangover.

I was cleaning up the breakfast dishes after having given Mum breakfast in bed. When Dad appeared somewhat sheepishly, I must have let out a sound of disgust because he said, 'What was that for?'

'You're joking, right?' I said.

'Is she going to be all right?'

'Yeah, no thanks to you.'

'Woman's a bloody fool to have taken those pills. I threw the rest of them away.'

'Oh, and you think that's all there is to it?'

He turned away from me and went to the teapot to pour himself some tea.

'Mum could have died! Dead, gone!'

'She wouldn't have died.'

'Of course she would have died. It was her last resort. A stupid effort to make you stop drinking! But I'm the idiot that I didn't see it coming. She warned you a thousand times to leave her alone. To stop tormenting her.'

'Silly bloody woman.'

'Yes! She is a silly bloody woman! For putting up with you! She should have walked out on you years ago.'

'You'd better watch what you're saying...'

'You can't hurt me any more. You might be able to hurt Mum but me, no. You're sad.'

He sat down and stirred his tea.

156

'What can I do?'

'What can you do? You're a smart man, Dad. We're living a nightmare here. The other kids are scared out of their wits.'

'Things'll get better.'

'They couldn't get any worse.'

He sat there, stirring and stirring the milk and sugar in his cup. I stood over him.

'I've decided to give up the booze.'

I headed out of the kitchen. 'I don't believe you.'

chapter 16

You give up a lot when you decide to compete in sports, especially at an international level. Your focus must be clear and single-minded. Mine was. I trained harder and harder. I never missed a training session in the morning or afternoon. I pushed myself.

Meanwhile, John did not. He took it easy.

I was determined after that first defeat that he would never beat me again. And he never did.

He quit high school at sixteen and began working full time. The fabric of our relationship was fraying, and I was no longer at ease with him. He started seeing a whole new group of friends and staying out late at night.

He joined a life-saving club and was participating in surf swimming and surf carnivals on a regular basis. He was popular and won lots of surfing races but this did not leave him a lot of time for the gruelling training sessions in the pool. Plus, his newfound sense of freedom was hard to give up. Beautiful girls thronged to the beaches on weekends and ogled the handsome lifeguards. Small wonder that John did not think much about competitive swimming.

I still did.

In 1961, I won my first Australian Open Championship in the one hundred metres. I came second in the two hundred metres, centimetres behind my nemesis, Julian Carroll, the New South Wales Champion. John competed but finished fourth. It was doubly gratifying that the 1961 Championships were held in Brisbane.

Dad did not come to see me achieve this long-awaited goal. When we returned home on the night I won, Dad was seated at the kitchen table, his usual spot when he was drinking. He was not especially drunk but he had a buzz on nevertheless. We all walked in in a high state of excitement.

'We have an Australian Champion in the family!' Mum said.

'Good on you, kid,' he said.

'That's it?' Mum said, '"Good on you, kid"?'

'What do you want me to say?' Dad asked.

'You've been pushing these boys since they were little kids to do what Tony has just done. You didn't even bother to come and see him do it.'

'I'm finished with all that swimming stuff,' he said.

He got up and went to get another bottle from the refrigerator. Mum took him by the arm and turned him to face her.

'What has he ever done to you?'

'Leave me alone,' he replied.

He took the bottle and walked to the back stairs and sat there, drinking from the bottle. Mum looked at me. I was fine. I was free of him and it felt good.

'Let's go to bed,' I said.

'Not even a little drink to celebrate?' Mum asked.

I looked at her and tapped the side of my head. 'I'll celebrate up here.'

I lay in bed in my own little circle of contentment. I was excited. I had achieved my life-long goal and it was thrilling. I was the best in Australia at something. But what now? Where was it taking me? I knew that the British Empire and Commonwealth Games were coming up and I wanted to be in them. It meant another long year of hard work and training but I was prepared to do it.

It must have been after midnight when I heard it. It was an odd noise, almost a cry, not quite a whimper. I sat up in bed. The others were all asleep. Then I heard it again. It was coming from the kitchen. It was a noise so difficult to place, and as I remember it now, one of the saddest sounds I've ever heard. It was all anguish.

I got up and went to the kitchen. There was its nightly resident in his nightly spot. Bent over in that curious way he had of sitting when he was drinking and thinking. His upper body almost on his thighs, a smouldering cigarette hanging from his fingers. There was a smell of flat or spilt beer, mixed with cigarette smoke. A smell I had grown to loathe.

Dad looked up at me as I came in.

'I heard a noise. Are you all right?' I said to my father.

'Yeah, I'm fine.' He looked down again at his feet.

'There was such a weird sound.'

Dad looked at me again. His eyes were red. If I didn't know any better I would have said that he'd been crying. But his eyes were often red from the drinking.

'Is there anything I can do for you?' I asked.

He shook his head. I turned to go out of the room.

'Tony...'

I stopped and turned back. His eyes were boring through me. But the sadness in them was so intense that I felt a powerful urge to go to him and pick him up and hug him.

'...Go to bed,' he said.

I headed to my bedroom. I came back to the kitchen with my gold medal. I placed it on the table in front of him. 'Dad, look at this.'

Blearily, he looked at the medal and nodded. Then he picked up his beer and took a slug from it. 'Hmmm.'

'It's the top of the heap, Dad! I'm the best backstroke swimmer in Australia. One of the best in the world!'

If he wouldn't pick it up, I would. I held it inches from his face.

'I've worked so hard for this. Given up so much. Tried so hard. This is for all of us. For Mum, the other kids, for you, Dad. So you'd be proud. So you'd be pleased.'

'Number one in Australia, eh?'

'Yes!' I almost shouted it. 'I wish it could have been a gold medal in football but they don't give gold medals in football and even if they did, I would never get one. And I didn't have much of a shot as a welterweight, that's for sure.'

I thought that might bring some flicker of recognition.

That a slight smile might cross his face. There was not a flicker of anything.

'I'm sorry you had such a tough life as a kid,' I said. 'I know the Depression was hard. I'm sorry you didn't play football for Australia. But Dad, this is *my* life. *My* success. And I'm going to make the most of it.'

Another swig of beer. I sat down on one of the chairs at the table.

'Funny little quirk of fate, isn't it?' I said finally, to plug the gap of silence. 'That it's me who's done this. I know you wanted Harold to play football for Australia. And I know you wanted John to get to the top in swimming. But it's me, Dad. Me.'

'Nothing to do with me.'

I picked up the medal and held it out again.

'I'm the Australian Champion and nobody, not even you, can take it away from me. Take it! I want you to have it.'

There was no response. I dropped the medal on the table. I stood up. The longing to connect was so great that I felt a deep pain. I turned from him and went back to my bed.

John dropped out of competitive swimming. I seemed to have the path to myself. In the 1962 Australian

Championships, I finished second in both the one hundred metres and the two hundred metres by only fractions of a second in both events. But this guaranteed me a position in the Australian training squad for the Empire and Commonwealth Games to be held later that year in Western Australia. The squad was selected to train in Ayr in Northern Queensland to escape the winter. We did nothing but train, eat and sleep and be totally pampered for four months in preparation for November. Don Talbot was the official coach.

Three weeks prior to the games themselves, trials were to be held in Melbourne. I was in the best shape of my life.

And then it happened again. John decided to compete in the trials. He came to Melbourne, once again having been trained in Brisbane by our father. It was his last shot at an Australian blazer.

This was difficult for Mum. She confided in me that she felt enormous conflict, even though I believe she hoped I would win. Somehow, she said, she thought I deserved to. Diane joined in. 'It's an unbearable situation,' she said. 'You've worked so hard for it and yet it would be nice for John, too.'

'I don't want to think about competing with John again,' I said. 'I hate it.'

In the one hundred metres, I was once again edged out by a fingernail by Julian Carroll but John, to his enormous credit and to my great pride, finished third, making it seem that a place on the team was assured for him as well, three to be chosen in each event. In the two hundred metres, his lack of training and stamina showed. He finished fourth.

The team was announced at the end of the trials that night. I stood with him as the names were read out. His name was not on the list. We looked at each other for a long time. It was his turn to be devastated as I had been a few years before. He was broken, his spirit shattered. I took him to one side, away from the curious eyes of all the other competitors. As we walked to a quiet spot, I thought of the many hard years since we were kids when swimming had been fun.

'It's a long way from the days of diving for pennies at Spring Hill,' I said.

John nodded and looked down, not wanting to cry.

'I wanted you to make the team,' I said to him. 'I wanted it with all my heart.'

He then buried his head in my shoulder and began to weep. 'I know you did,' he said.

I was completely taken aback. I didn't know whether to pat his back, hug him or do nothing. I gave him a short hug and then pushed him a little from me. I didn't know if I could find my voice. 'It's what we always thought and hoped would happen, isn't it? Since you won that first Under-Twelve Championship, I dreamed of us both representing Australia. I never dared think I would ever make it but I always thought you would.'

'You wanted it more. And you worked harder for it,' he said.

I didn't know what more I could say. 'Try not to take this too hard. Promise me. I know Dad pressured you into it. When I first saw you in the same race, I thought, well...I thought it was the end of the world. I wish I'd known what was going on. Why didn't you tell me?'

'Dad didn't want me to.'

'I'd have told you. Since then it hasn't been the same, has it?'

'Dad thought it was the only way I could win.'

I nodded. 'It wasn't the end of the world for me then and it isn't the end of the world for you now. There are other things besides swimming.'

We were both silent.

'I want us to be friends again,' I went on. 'The way we used to be. You're my brother and I love you. After this is all over...'

I held out my hand to shake his. To do our silly

handshake for old times' sake. John did not take it.

'You mean after you go to the Empire Games and I don't?'

'Well, yeah, I mean...'

'You're so bloody noble, aren't you? Saint bloody Tony.' He stood up. 'You got every bloody thing you wanted. I didn't. Dad promised me that I'd go to the Games. Not you. He said it didn't matter about you.'

In November 1962, I competed in the Empire Games in Perth. I finished second in the two hundred metres. I had a silver medal. Second, second, second! I was determined that I would have a gold in the one hundred to be held two days later. I had a new game plan.

But in the end I outsmarted myself. I decided to go out faster than usual on the first lap. I was a long way ahead of the other seven competitors at the end of fifty metres. But I misjudged the turn. My feet didn't even touch the wall and I couldn't push off. The other swimmers caught up to me as I floundered around. Though I actually finished third, I was disqualified for not touching the end in the turn.

I have swum that race in my head a million times. But something more important than winning a silver medal happened at the Empire Games. It changed my life forever.

chapter 17

I trained harder than ever after the letdown of the Empire Games. Back again in Perth in February 1963, I won two Australian Championships. First for a change. But by now, I had another dream.

During the Empire Games, I'd roomed with Murray Rose. Murray won three gold medals in Melbourne in 1956 and one at the Rome Olympics in 1960, and at the Empire Games he won another two gold medals. Between Melbourne and Rome, he had won a scholarship to the University of Southern California in Los Angeles where he majored in drama, hoping to set himself up in a career as an actor in movies and television.

In Perth, I asked Murray all about this. What was involved? What could it achieve? He told me how he had applied to USC and been given a full scholarship for four years. I thought that sounded pretty good. But Murray Rose was Murray Rose. What American college would not want him to attend their school? Nonetheless, he told me how to go about applying.

In 1963, John Kennedy was in the White House. Kennedy had gone to Harvard, the greatest university in America. John Kenneth Galbraith and Henry Kissinger taught there. I thought John Kennedy was the most charismatic and brilliant politician in the world. At the risk of mixing my metaphors, Harvard seemed to me like Oz at the end of the yellow brick road.

With encouragement and help from Murray, I applied to a mysterious sounding person called the Dean of Admissions, Harvard University, Cambridge, Massachusetts, USA. A few weeks later, I received a friendly and encouraging letter from the Dean and an envelope containing a thousand and one forms, which I filled in and returned. And waited. Was this what I had dreamed and hoped might happen to me after all my swimming? Not even remotely. It fell out of the sky and I grabbed at it. In April, I received another letter. It began: 'Dear Mr Fingleton: I am delighted to inform you that the Committee of Admissions and Financial Aid has voted to offer you a place in the class of 1967. Please accept our personal congratulations for your outstanding achievements.'

I was not familiar with the American way of naming classes for the year in which students graduated but I was quickly able to work out that in 1967, four years from then, I would have a degree from Harvard.

As we sat around the dinner table that night, I could see that my news was not so thrilling to others in my family.

My mother was distraught. 'Why on earth would you want to do a thing like that? What do you want to go to America for?'

'Your mother's right,' my father chimed in. 'What about the Olympics?'

'The Olympics?' I said. 'What about the Olympics?'

'Are you bloody deaf or something?' my father said. 'You've got a shot at being an Olympian.'

I found it disconcerting that my father was now interested in my swimming career.

'Of course, I'd love to go to the Olympics,' I said. 'But I can't do both. I'd rather go to Harvard. With this scholarship, I've achieved more than I ever thought possible. Much more than I would from going to the Olympics.'

'Stupidest bloody idea I've ever heard,' Dad said.

Mum was adamant. 'I don't want you to go.'

'I don't want you to go either,' Diane chimed in.

'I thought you'd understand.'

'Don't you see? It leaves *us*—here.'

Ronald too, was against it. 'We'll miss you too much if you go, mate.'

But I was determined. I would begin at Harvard in September 1963. I went about making plans to get there the cheapest way possible. I couldn't afford the air fare so I settled on a cargo vessel that was to take three weeks to cross the Pacific, go through the Panama Canal and then up the east coast of America and finally on to Boston.

A few days before I was to sail, we all went to the beach. I wanted to have one last swim in the surf and to enjoy the beauty of Surfers Paradise. Mum was becoming more and more introverted. I knew it was going to be hard on her. As I came out of the surf, I found her sitting on a bench alone, staring out to sea. I sat down beside her and pointed towards the water.

'America's as far as you can go straight ahead and a bit to the left.'

She was not amused.

'Don't make a joke of it,' she said.

'I have to go. I can't turn my back on this.'

'But I'm going to miss you so much. We all will. What about Diane? She looks up to you so much. Even your father will miss you.'

I shot her a look. 'Now, you're joking,' I said.

'He will,' she said. 'I think he's finally coming to grips with the fact that he must pay a price for being an absentee father to you.'

'It's only for four years. Say it quickly and it doesn't sound like such a long time. It's not forever.'

'It might be.'

I put my arm around her. 'Mum, you're my hero, did you know that?'

She burst into tears. She took my hands in hers and, in a little action that she had done so many times during my life, wiped the top of my hand with her handkerchief. Back and forth. First one hand, then the other.

Finally, I broke the silence. 'I've never known what I was going to do with my life. I've never had a real plan. I think that's why I clung so hard to swimming. I thought, in some strange way, it would take me by the hand and lead me somewhere. That something would come of it. And now I think it has.'

'Look what all your swimming got me,' she said. 'I've lost a son as a result.'

She ran her hand along the side of my face. 'Harvard! I wonder if you'll see President Kennedy...'

'You never know. Mum, will you be okay?'

'I'm a little afraid, that's all.'

'Of what?'

'Of myself. Of the future.'

'Mum, you're the one who told me not to be afraid of the future,' I said.

She looked at me hard, knowing I was right. 'I always knew those words would come back to haunt me.'

Ships take forever to pull away from a wharf. We waved and shouted inanities to each other and my mother cried—for almost an hour! It might have been comic if there hadn't been an undertone of despair to it. I knew what she was thinking. What would the future hold for her and her life with Dad? Was I running away from it?

chapter 18

I'd like to think that time heals all wounds. It doesn't though. It tatters the edges of memory and softens the focus. But I think if the wounds are deep enough, maybe you don't ever really get over them.

I swam for one year on the Harvard team and quit. I explained to the swimming coach that I had been going up and down swimming pools since I was eleven and I was bored. He was disappointed but understanding. I have not missed the smell of chlorine one little bit.

I graduated from Harvard on 15 June 1967 and married Pam in Boston the following day. We moved to

New York where we raised our two daughters. I started a career writing for the screen and stage.

John married shortly before I left but the marriage did not last more than three years. He remarried and moved to Sydney. The estrangement that began those many years ago on the blocks of the Valley pool has only widened and we no longer keep in touch.

Ronald and Diane still lived at home, teenagers, both still studying and then working. They coped with the grind of Dad's and Harold's routine bouts with the bottle, Ronald by throwing himself into sports and Diane by focusing on her studies. During high school, Ronald was a star athlete—rugby union, cricket, swimming and hurdles. He has been married twice and has three children.

Harold married and had a son, Marc, but the marriage failed after several years. When the marriage broke up, Harold moved back into Mum and Dad's house. Eventually, he decided to give up drinking and Diane's support of his decision was gallant.

As I had, Diane spread her wings and took flight. Not long after finishing secondary school, she travelled overseas. She settled in New York for three years or so and it was wonderful to have her close by. In 1972, she returned home to begin a new life in Australia.

When Diane was living overseas and when Ronald got married, Mum was on her own with Dad. During that time, Ronald and his wife would receive calls to go over to Mum and Dad's to help Mum because she was afraid for her life. On one occasion, they arrived to find Mum being held at bay by Dad with an axe.

Upon her return to Australia, Diane realised that they must be separated, or else there would be a tragedy—either Dad would kill Mum or Mum would succeed in suicide.

Diane found a flat for Mum. Dad also moved into a flat. Their accumulated assets were sold to a second-hand dealer—there wasn't much of value there but it was all they had.

Eventually, Mum and Dad made peace with each other. Once Dad moved to his flat, strangely, his need to drink subsided and he stopped—for good. Some time after Mum and Dad had separated, they were both eligible to move into Housing Commission flats, which they did. They were some suburbs away from each other but they stayed in constant touch.

Diane began a career that would involve her as an assistant to the Treasurer of Australia. She then studied law and upon graduating, spent several years in legal aid work. In due course, she was made a judge and has recently been appointed the Chief Magistrate of the state of Queensland. She married 'her John' as she calls him and is as happy as anyone I know.

Mum was inconsolable when Dad died in August 1985, aged seventy-six. I didn't tell her that I found that strange, given all that she had been through with him. They had an amazing bond which I am at a loss to comprehend fully. I remember an odd little game they used to play when they sat at the kitchen table. Dad had a silly habit of stirring his hot tea, taking out the spoon and pretending to touch Mum's arm with it—instead he would touch her with his index finger. She would jump, berate him slightly, knowing that he was not going to scald her with his spoon. It was a flirtation—a sign of feeling good about each other—which meant peace and happiness in the house.

Memory has a peculiar capability of distorting facts and reshaping events. Perhaps my memories are not consistent with the events as my brothers and Diane remember them and they will be surprised by much of what I have written here. Perhaps Dad never meant to hurt me as much as I felt he did. He doesn't seem to have hurt my brothers in quite the same way. He claimed in his later years that he did not mean to hurt me or, indeed, know that he had.

I suppose we're all revisionists to some extent. We often choose to remember what we want to remember. But perhaps Dad truly had no idea how tough it was to be his son. The son who perhaps needed more of what kindness there was in his heart. Perhaps it didn't matter to him. Whether it was his intention to hurt, or whether it is my distortion of reality that I feel he hurt me so much, is sometimes hard to keep entirely clear.

There is no enmity in my heart. Nor do I feel anger. Anger was what Dad had.

I have tried to be as factual as I could. And not just about the facts of our lives together as I remember them. Factual in my head and factual in my heart as well.

I'm grateful that Dad tried, in his way, to give us the semblance of a family life totally unlike what he himself had had as a young person. He worked hard and provided us with a roof over our heads and food on the table during our important early years. He didn't have that. We each had the education we sought. I'll always be grateful that he pushed us into competitive swimming.

After Dad died, Mum's health began to decline precipitously. Then, in the second half of 1988 she was diagnosed with stomach cancer. I telephoned her often and was distraught that I could not be closer. At this time, a play I had co-written was produced in the West End of London at the Savoy Theatre. It was a thrilling experience. Donald Sinden played the male lead, but more significant to me was the fact that June Whitfield played the female lead—whom I had named Dora Winslow as a little homage to Mum. I called Mum to tell her.

'You'll never guess who's going to be in my play in London—playing Dora,' I said to her.

'Who is it, darling?'

'June Whitfield! Remember? She was Eth in "Take It From Here"! The radio. We listened to it every Sunday night!'

She remembered. 'Oh, how marvellous, love. Remember that funny whiny way she used to say, "Oh, Ron"? Do you think you can ask her to do her "Oh, Ron" voice?'

'I'll ask her. I'll tell her it's for you.'

'"Take It From Here"', she said. 'That takes me back. To Boundary Street.'

'And "The Hit Parade" and "Inner Sanctum" and...'

'"The Search For The Golden Boomerang"'.

My brothers and Diane took wonderful care of Mum during her final days. I flew over to be with her for as long as I could but was not there at the end. Before I left for the airport, I sat quietly with her and tried to compress in a few moments the entirety of our life together. But she was too ill to say much. I sat beside her on her bed and wiped her forehead and held her hands— the way she had done to me so often when I was young and sick a lot. I looked at her, and tears welled up in my eyes. She was my Mum. I was this big hulking adult person but she was still my Mum. And she was dying. And we both knew it. She didn't cry. I couldn't stop.

She died three weeks later. It was an unbearable sadness for us all.

For years I never went near a swimming pool. I kept fit by jogging around the reservoir in New York's Central Park, until the legs gave out. Then, I discovered a fifty-metre swimming pool, a short bicycle ride from my New York apartment. I can't believe it, but I now enjoy getting up to swim two miles each morning at five-thirty.

Sometimes, especially in the dead of winter or peak of summer, I open my eyes in the morning and I do not want to get out of my bed. It's too cold. It's too hot. And then the image of my father pops into my head. He is standing at our bedroom door in Spring Hill. 'Time to get up. Let's go.'

Some days, I almost murmur, 'Okay, Dad, I'll show them.'

I get up. I do it.

'You might fool me,' I hear him say, 'but you can't fool yourself.'

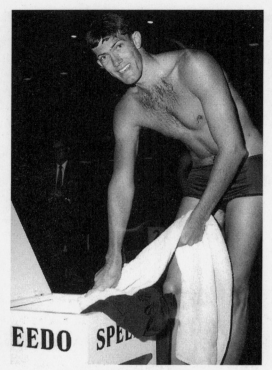

AT THE MELBOURNE OLYMPIC POOL,
SHORTLY BEFORE THE EMPIRE GAMES

acknowledgments

The saga of writing this book and subsequent movie rivals the events that are depicted in it. The book and screenplay have been many years in the writing and through many, many drafts. Whole forests have been cleared to provide the paper that has been used to print up its pages.

I want to thank my brothers Harold, John and Ronald who lived through our troubled youth with me. I share so many memories with them. And of course, with Diane.

I have leaned on so many friends for advice and help for so long that I am sure they will be thankful that it has finally gone to press.

My daughter Samantha gave me the title. My daughter Priscilla was there with my sister Diane and me when this all got aborning.

My friend George Malko listened and suggested and tolerated and knew.

My friend Carlos Davis has heard every story contained herein a hundred times and in a hundred different variations. And always with wisdom and, more importantly, with good humour.

My friend David Taylor (the professor) is wise and kind and thoughtful and helpful. When he said so many times, 'Spare me no detail,' I didn't and he listened and supported.

Lynn Bayonas helped me organise my haphazard thoughts and stories and gave me the courage to dig deeper into my heart and into the hurt.

Howard and Karen Baldwin saw the movie in the book and made sure others would see it too.

My agent Maggie Field and lawyer Jamie Feldman kept me from jumping over the brink.

Michael Heyward was the only publisher I ever wanted to publish this book. He has read so many versions of it and knows more about me than he probably has a right to—without charging me a psychiatrist's fee.

Thanks to my wife Pam. She's lived with me through the adventure that is *Swimming Upstream* and the adventure otherwise known as *Our Lives*. I am nothing without her.

But most of all to Mum and Dad who, in their way, did what they could to give us as much as they were capable of. Not always wisely and not always well. But I am who I am because of these two extraordinary ordinary people.